Signs of Madness

David Arthur Walters

Published by David Arthur Walters, 2024.

SIGNS OF MADNESS

First edition. November 22, 2024.

ISBN: 979-8227653741

Written by David Arthur Walters.

Also by David Arthur Walters

The Seed That Fell On Rocky Ground
South Beach Florida Coronavirus Panic 2020
The Yellow Vest Movement
Signs of Madness
The Compassionate Heart of America
My Hawaii Nei
The Amazing South Beach HDD Sewer Project
Tracey's Secret
The Amazing Kansas City Library
The Helgalian Chronicles
The Espanola Way of Doing Business
Katherine Sergava
No Hard Feelings - A Dancer's Reflections
Sovereign Immunity - The Debasement of the United States
Helene and Paul - A Characterological Romance
Anarkhia
Random Ramblings
Melange
Ideology aka Idiotology
Accounts Payable - My Life Past Due
The Sly Way Gurdjieff & Ouspensky
Groundhog Days - Timely Intercourse
The Black VIrgin
APXH - Wicked Political Musings
Open Publishing
My Hand

Table of Contents

Introduction

I have always loved to write for the sake of writing because I always learned a great deal in the process. I aspired to be a journalist instead of an academic writer and short story teller after I moved to Kansas City to take care of my ailing father, and then on to Miami Beach. The newspaper editors in the Heart of America and in the Miami Area were not interested in hiring self-taught journalists no matter how good or promising they might be, nor were city officials interested in making official use of my skills.

That is, with the exception of a little free sidewalk paper in Miami Beach, called the SunPost, whose editor published a great deal of my work on official negligence and moral if not criminal corruption in the construction industry until she got an email from the city attorney defaming me and insisting I be blackballed. She complied for political reasons, saying I was a "wild card." Oh, yes, there was an online news outlet whose editor wanted to take me on with the condition I did not write anything about certain sensitive subjects he was involved in. I was mad but undaunted by rejection.

No local disorder has been too insignificant to be unworthy of the application of my talent for research and reporting, starting with unpermitted signs, unleashed dogs, and unruly bicycling. This is a collection of some of my work on those subjects. Although I was an instrument of some reform in those minor areas, I think, now that I reflect on this collection near the end of my life, that I may have gone quite mad, or that I have always been mad, obsessed with studying and writing instead of leading what is called a "productive" life. Therefore the title, *Signs of Madness*.

Signs of Impending Doom

Our high civilization suffers a mortal infectious disease transmitted and aggravated by mass communication based on the fetish for dead objects and the pernicious perseveration of vicious imagery taken out of context. As social animals we have a tendency to imitate, and the media is our main guide.

Ironically, the media executives and lobbyists who deny the harmful consequences of violent communications rely for success on positive affirmations and attitudes, on mottoes and slogans, visions, mission statements, success stories and other prayers. Of course, the petitions are for net profit, thus the vicious cycle is perpetuated.

One sort of prosperity, such as net profit or savings, pursued as the purpose of life, constitutes the worst kind of spiritual poverty. "Stocks" were once sticks on which accounts were kept. Now too many of us have become economic ants carrying our stocks on our backs up the wall of financial worry, a wall where our big gun, that is, our collective defense, Humpty Dumpty, uselessly awaits us.

The period of sustained economic growth that appears to satisfy the few, but does not fully satiate their desires is a horrible hell to others who need viable alternatives to check the waves of random violence that are bound to encircle the insane global pursuit of dead objects and the mutual contempt of competitors.

Observe the obsession with violent images thrown with wanton disregard into the pool of life. The rebounding waves of virtual, redundant violence are amassing at that critical point where image is converted into accelerating action, threatening to destroy us in an orgy of mass murder-suicide.

SIGNS OF MADNESS

What other signs do we have of the coming cataclysm besides raving prophets, lying leaders, school and church and nightclub shootings, terrorist acts including the mass murder of civilians in wars, and mounting prison populations? When shall we be sure that the end time is near, that the final period is upon us? There are many signs everywhere, creeping up on us through the cracks in all walks of life. We are unaware that the doom of our civilization is nigh because many of us have been persuaded that history is merely the evolution of technology.

The fact that our democracy is now an economic dictatorship feeding on the carcass of the spiritual body is seldom mentioned by professionals; what counts is that the colossal maggot feeds efficiently. Technology preachers presume to tell us what we will want next; efficiency is the idol, so everyone must have a personal digital assistant to distract him from his slavery with an illusion of freedom, and have a life otherwise bemused and bewitched by gimmicks and gadgets.

The efficient exploitation of public opinion reigns supreme; there are no longer leaders of public opinion; there are only imitators and exploiters of it. Techno-capitalists produce the circumstances of our lives, which we live out as zombies under a coercive technological totalitarianism sponsored by the big business state.

Voters idolize rich candidates, imagining they can make their dreams come true no matter how contradictory the promises may be. Consciences are sold cheaply at market prices.

When the government, which is supposed to have a monopoly on violent means, does not use its power to disarm individuals for the public good or protect them from nuclear attack, it seems that private firearms will indeed be needed to protect us, not so much from the usual suspects, but from governments that are organized crime legalized.

Yes, many are the signs of the impending doom. Some seem rather trivial. When the distances between periods diminishes; when sentences get shorter and shorter; when word processing programs dictate sentence length and otherwise shrink consciousness into mechanical definitions of good grammar; when attention spans are so short that only sound bites will do; when conversations sound like machine guns spitting out uniform bullets; when delightful romantic discourse can no longer be carried on; and when everyone talks technology: these are just a few of the incidental signs along the fast road to doom.

What we observe in the prophecies of doom and in the popular movies about natural disasters and random violence is not only a death wish; it is a dying plea for the restoration of a proper balance between fear and love. Between fear and love there must be the faith that there is a greater good, a higher good than state or society, regardless of its denomination. The progress from fear through faith to love may be contemplated, in the form of a convenient over-simplification, in terms of ages.

The age of fear is the rule of law under the state. The age of faith is the beneficence of grace within the church. The age of love is the intercourse of free society. The progression is from slavery to voluntary obedience to freedom; under the objective forms of monarchy, aristocracy, and democracy; as personalized by the relations of father, mother, and children; the relatives are essentially one family. All are one and one is all. The differences perceived are perspectival.

If we do not broaden our perspectives and restore the proper relation of fear, faith, and love, if restitution is not forthcoming soon, the prophet will keep ranting that the violent images before us are self-fulfilling prophecies, that our death wish will come true sooner than we think, and that we will surely receive what we ask for. Doom.

Signs of Madness

The few friends I have left, if there are any left, may think that I have gone completely mad given my recent obsession with violations of the city's signage ordinances. For weeks now I have been perambulating the city, taking pictures of unpermitted signs, and sending them along to city officials, insisting that the fact that sign laws are going unenforced is a sign of a permissive regulatory culture that is bound to doom the city absent an immediate crackdown.

If anything, I am a victim of obsessive compulsive signage disorder (OCSD). The city attorney believes that I am delusional, that I suffer from what the Soviet psychiatrists called "sluggish schizophrenia" for not realizing that I live under the best of all city governments: a weak-mayor, strong city manager, fascistic government. He does not appreciate my struggle for truth and honesty in government, which was the only obvious sign of the Soviet disease. Indeed, he has publicly pronounced me a signal moron or town fool. Not that he believes I am unintelligent, or that I am not a genius, but that I am a damn fool for not understanding how things are best done in his town. That is why he told me twice that I would not be around his town for long.

Yes, I am from out of town. So is he, but southern Florida is the northern province of his motherland, Cuba, whereas I am a gringo or foreigner in my own nation, a damn Yankee and resented Americano in a state Uncle Sam grabbed from Spain and Indians. I am dumb in the dumb sense that Hawaiians called haoles dumb after the foreigners settled in the islands, and haoles likewise called Hawaiians "dumb Hawaiians."

However, if I become fluent in Spanish and fit into the local culture, no one will be the any wiser in these parts. Northerners think we are all stupid down here, and they may be right. I used to call locals stupid until I started doing stupid things and realized that stupidity is contagious. Thankfully, the more we realize how stupid we are, the wiser we shall be, at least according to Socrates.

The city manager, according to a Parks Department employee, did not call me stupid but he declared me "crazy" shortly after I arrived in his paradise, because I criticized what he called a few bad blades of grass in his great lawn, and wrote a story about a hole in the ground in South Pointe Park beside Government Cut, a big hole that had been covered by an overgrowth of weeds. A scantily dressed young lady with a hangover and a Blackberry, whom I had met on the beach very early in the morning after the Food Fair, and whose name I shall not disclose because she was the runaway daughter of a high state official, nearly broke her leg when it plunged into the hole up to her hip.

I capitalized the hole as 'The Hole,' and reported on the incident because, in the Big Apple at least, when a hole is reported and someone else gets hurt by it, the city is liable for damages. After The Hole was filled some months later, the filling mysteriously disappeared, and I speculated in my follow-up report that it was one end of a tunnel used by chupacabras in Puerto Rico to visit South Beach. It was more probably the work of crabs.

A tourist drowned in a hole right off the beach at Lincoln Road in broad daylight not long thereafter, on a holiday when the beach was crowded with tourists. His little children stood by dumbfounded as Beach Rescue tried to save their dad to no avail. Mom was waiting in a hotel room for their return. Local media rejected my story on the incident and it was not otherwise reported. I called a lawyer for the plaintiff in a drowning that had occurred further up the beach. He said the legislature had changed the rules on governmental liability because he was winning, and a lot of taxpayer money was at stake due to drownings along the Florida coastline.

A lifeguard contacted me to say that the city manager's office had advised lifeguards not to talk to the "crazy" journalist, namely me. The lifeguard attributed the tragedy I had witnessed to a blind spot between lifeguard stations, which I capitalized as 'The Blind Spot' in my subsequent report.

Furthermore, some stations along "chic" South Beach had been damaged by storms, and were being used nightly as shooting galleries and toilets. Lifeguards rebuilt one destroyed station from scrap wood. He said taking up the issue with the city manager would be to no avail because the city manager was stingy and did not want to build and staff another lifeguard station. He asked me to deliver a copy of my report to the only commissioner whom he said really cared about regular people—she would become mayor and the manager's best friend.

Several lifeguard stations were repaired or replaced. One of them, at the south end of the beach, built in the form of a lighthouse, has become a national sign for South Beach. However, during a visit to the Planning Department at the end of the year, I was informed that it and the other stations were soon to be replaced by structures designed by the same architect who designed the original structures destroyed in the storms.

I forewarned the foremost South Pointe activist of the alleged plan so that he could organize a Save the Lifeguard Lighthouse movement, but he did not respond, perhaps because he is more interested in trash on the beach than sending out a signal to tourists that could be interpreted as a warning that they might be shipwrecked and drowned unless they steer clear of the beach. Flooding is in fact a big issue in these parts, and Miami Beach could be the first to realize Al Gore's inconvenient truth that the overbuilt Florida coast is doomed because of the stolen presidency.

I accepted the new Lifeguard Lighthouse within the park because I found my long-lost sister and she loves lighthouses, but I really do not care much for change. President Clinton said we should all Welcome Change, and President Obama advocated a big CHANGE, but I do not want to be a welcome mat for other people's changes. I prefer Plato's permanent ideas to the ephemeral things of this best of all possible worlds, and think most things are best left alone once food, shelter, mates, and Internet access are obtained. Why must we insist on filling the world with more and more trash, junk, and garbage to increase gross production and consumption?

So I did not approve of the rehabilitation of South Pointe Park at first. I made an exception for the Lifeguard Lighthouse on the beach, but I did not care for the staggered column of the lighthouse sculpture now surrounded by dog waste in the park. Ironically, my father's ashes were scattered in the water nearby before it became a protested dog park. He did not care much for dogs himself; he said they should be canned and shipped to the Philippines to feed the poor.

As for the iceberg sculptures capping off the restrooms the park, I thought they represented the frozen hearts of politicians who forced the renovation down the throats of frustrated conservatives.

However, I have had a change of heart. I even recommended to the mayor that the park be renamed after the city manager who oversaw the project. Sadly, that cannot be done until he is dead and permanent gone—his return is feared by the current regime, faux reformists who advocated welcome changes, some of whom may have secretly wished him dead. I have often enjoyed South Pointe Park since his departure even though the walkway has become too crowded during my Sunday morning walks. But its popularity among the gentility, who are better off than the gentuza who fished there before, has provided me with the opportunity to cover two robberies around the icebergs in the last three Sundays. Of course there is always a story to be told about something wherever I go.

I espied two women photographing a model in his blue underpants on the iceberg deck last Sunday. It was suitably icy on the deck so all but he were warmly clad. He lacked the prerequisite of barbarian comeliness: a hirsute physique notwithstanding a bald pate evidencing abundant testosterone.

Barbarians, as we know, hail from the north, where they were created by the iceberg gods. Most men, since they left jungle and forest, prefer their females rather hairless, and small for the sake of portability, hence evolution has rendered them relatively small and hairless in comparison to males, whose brute power gave them no cause to shed their own hair but to flaunt it and grow in stature. Conservative men certainly do not remove from their bodies what little hair they may have been blessed with, a fact that is greatly appreciated by a tactile Cherokee woman I met on a train from Chicago to New York City back in the good old days when I let my undergrowth run wild.

"Do you ladies need a model with a hairy chest, hairy legs, and hairy belly?" I asked the photographers, but they demurred, and their model giggled. What is this world coming to?

Maybe I complain too much. I admit that I have complained a lot about the present state of many things, therefore my objections to change unless they are my changes are hypocritical. I have learned from the admission of my own hypocrisy in comparison to others that hypocrisy is the underlying crisis of human nature. We are not all that we would be, and we are moved to lie about who we are and to complain about what other people do or do not do.

In fact, complaining is the lever of human progress, so people are welcome to blame me for complaining, especially about government, and to send me one dollar each. My dad said, understandingly, that I had a "conflict with authority." We all have a bit of that, without which we would not be a people destined for freedom in order.

Now in the old days, those of the Athenian democracy, there were no regular public prosecutors. Citizens could volunteer to file complaints on behalf of the public. It was said private wrongs resulted in public goods. We democrats have not changed much since Athens. Now that an official sniveler has threatened to slap me with a defamation suit for doing what he has done to me, I sympathize with the predicament Aeschines spoke of in his speech against Timarchus, and am fain to defend myself:

"I have never, fellow citizens, brought indictment against any Athenian, nor vexed any man when he was rendering account of his office; but in all such matters I have, as I believe, shown myself a quiet and modest man. But when I saw that the city was being seriously injured by the defendant, Timarchus, who, though disqualified by law, was speaking in your assemblies [he later argues that Timarchus should have been disqualified by unethical behavior from practicing law], and when I myself was made a victim of his blackmailing attack the nature of the attack I will show in the course of my speech, I decided that it would be a most shameful thing if 1 failed to come to the defense of the whole city and its laws, and to your defense and my own; and knowing that he was liable to the accusations that you heard read a moment ago by the clerk of the court, I instituted this suit, challenging him to official scrutiny. Thus it appears, fellow citizens, that what is so frequently said of public suits is no mistake, namely, that very often private enmities correct public abuses."

In any case, if someone simply had a grudge against someone back then for which there was no civil remedy, he could sue him for some crime or the other. Of course that process was abused by informers called "sycophants" for giving the finger or "showing the fig" to someone while flattering the public that they were taking action for its good.

Now I admit that I have shown the fig to various authorities including local officials of the City of Miami Beach, lately in the form of sign code violations on every block, but not because I consider any official in particular as an enemy with whom I must get even. Mind you that it is they who have threatened to bring frivolous and malicious suits against me to shut me up.

The public naturally suspected that sycophants had ulterior motives, that they were wont to bring frivolous and malicious suits against their personal enemies. Aristophanes took them to task in his comedy named after the god of wealth, Plutus, in dialogue between Good Man and Informer.

Informer admitted to Good Man that he had no occupation other than being the caretaker of public and private affairs by informing the public of wrongdoing. My own version of Good Man, the city attorney or city sphinx who guards the city walls with sophisms, publicly compared me to an unemployed, unlicensed watchdog that stalks public officials and urinates in city-hall's hallways.

Yet I, like the ancient comic poet's Informer, naturally perceive myself to be one of the more honest and patriotic citizens of my cosmos. Just Man asks how Informer can be of any benefit by meddling in other people's business, and Informer replies that he does not meddle but rather benefits the public by supporting enacted laws by not permitting them to be broken. Well, are not judges appointed to handle litigation? Yes, but anyone who wishes can prosecute, answers our sycophant, and that person is me because I am concerned with affairs of state. Good Man then concludes that the state has a bad patron.

The modern state saved itself from such bad patrons by providing cooperative sycophants with a monopoly on the practice of law. Lawyers are licensed to extort and blackmail and defame people at will, and it is nearly impossible to hold them liable for abuse of process and malicious prosecution, provided that they flatter the public with their noble pretensions to save it from perdition with their sophistry.

#

One thing that really gripes me about Florida law is that lawyers are not required to put their license numbers on their signs and other advertisements like contractors, architects, and interior designers. Neither are engineers, but at least engineers must have official seals. Another pet peeve is that state officials do not enforce the license number requirement unless someone complains about the violations. The same goes for the temporary construction and real estate signage laws in the City of Miami Beach. Code enforcement officers ignore countless violations in front of their faces. Perhaps over half of the signs have no permits, and what is permitted often constitutes violations of signage design criteria. In fact, the signage scofflaws make walking down the street a horror for law-abiding citizens who happen to know what the laws are.

In fine, the disorder in signage advertisements in the City of Miami Beach is yet another sign of the general official negligence and permissiveness and money-mongering contempt for culture that is working *The Decline of the West* voluminously referred to by Oswald Arnold Gottfried Spengler

"There is a city-point, in which the whole life of broad regions is collecting while the rest dries up. In place of a type-true people, born of and grown on the soil, there is a new sort of nomad, cohering unstably in fluid masses, the parasitical city dweller, tradition-less, utterly matter-of-fact, irreligious, clever, unfruitful, and deeply contemptuous of the countryman. This is a very great stride towards the inorganic, towards the end."

Spengler recalls that "It was in the conception of money as an inorganic and abstract magnitude, entirely disconnected from the notion of the fruitful earth and the primitive values, that the Romans had the advantage of the Greeks. Thenceforward any high ideal of life becomes largely a question of money."

Of course those who count me mad believe that the impermissible signs and I find fault with and which blight nearly every city block are insignificant , not to mention the officials who tolerate them, They believe I am indeed obsessed with trivia, while I believe they are the signs of a decadent culture the likes of which has not been seen before the Flood, and which should give cause to intuitive denizens to recall the ancient warning of Gilgamesh to tear down the houses and use the wood to build rafts to save themselves from the inevitable.

I shall reveal to you, Gilgamesh, a thing that is hidden, a secret of the gods I shall tell you, about a city that you surely know, situated on the banks of the Euphrates. That city was very old, and there were gods inside it. The hearts of the great gods moved them to inflict the flood. Epic of Gilgamesh.

According to *The New Science* of Giambattista Vico, cultures arise again subsequent to universal floods when water evaporates leaving mud. Culture proceeds with the robust generation of barbarian giants grown in their own filth because their mothers were too busy searching for food to cleanse them. Gods are then re-invented in their image.

"For it took that much time to reduce the earth to such a state that, dry of the moisture of the universal flood, it could send up dry exhalations or matter igniting in the air to produce lightning. Thereupon a few giants, who must have been the most robust, and who were dispersed through the forests on the mountain heights where the strongest beasts have their dens, were frightened and astonished by the great effect whose cause they did not know, and raised their eyes and became aware of the sky. And because in such a case, as stated in the Axioms, the nature of the human mind leads it to attribute its own nature to the effect, and because in that state their nature was that of men all robust bodily strength, who expressed their very violent passions by shouting and grumbling, they pictured the sky to themselves as a great animated body, which in that aspect they called Jove, the first god of the so-called gentes maiores, who by the whistling of his bolts and the noise of his thunder was attempting to tell them something."

Widespread sophistry is a sure sign that The End is not only nigh but that it is welcome. Sophists make the worst scenes seem the best, scoff at authority, and make fools of gods, thus corrupting the youth. Take for example this comment I received from a young political activist:

"I am been thinking about the non-permitted signs. There is something not offensive about it, because everyone is breaking the law, poor, rich, well connected, those with no connections. No one gets special treatment because no one is given a violation. What really upsets me is when developers bribe code or bride elected officials, or when elected officials give special treatment to their rich buddies or family members."

Thus has the community sunk to its lowest level, that the common denominator, the arbitrary, anarchic individual may rule. We have in this city by the beach a plight similar to that of Athens of old, where, as we learn from an introduction to Aristophanes' Clouds (*Introduction to Aristophanes' Clouds*, edited by M.W. Humpreys, Boston: Ginn, Heath, & Co 1885), "There is a time when criticism takes the place of unbounded and submissive confidence in what is usual, and calls into question the grounds of the existing state of affairs. Such an age begins for Hellas, and especially for Athens, with the Peloponnesian war. Slow in growth, this age was long-lived. Within, the frequent changes of forms of government by which the entire people was brought to participate in public affairs, without, the comparatively sudden and wide extension of trade and commerce, the ever growing acquaintance with strange countries and states, had exercised great influence in directing attention to differences of customs, and in lifting the judgment concerning such things to a more elevated and comprehensive standpoint. Then the progress of democratic principles, accelerated by the elevation of the people in the Persian wars, gave a lively impulse to the spirit of opposition, and made readiness to speak and reply on the spur of the moment an indispensable condition to participation in state affairs.... For the individual, especially among the educated, every previously respected barrier was giving way; what had stood firm was becoming unstable and doubtful. Law, faith, religion had claims only so far as they were recognized by the individual. The freest play was given to criticism, criticism of the most frivolous character, such as is nothing more than a whim of the fancy. Every united effort, everything that had, as a firm bond, held the state together, was relaxed by doubt. The foundations of society were shaken; and in case of a more general dissemination of such principles, enlightenment would have succumbed to the worst sort of barbarism, - egotistic individualism and want of character.

Superficial as the unpermitted signs may be, they are nevertheless a sure sign of widespread depravity behind the scenes. No less than the Clouds are at fault for the deplorable state of affairs. And who are the Clouds?

"They are the Clouds of heaven, great goddesses for the lazy; to them we owe all, thoughts, speeches, trickery, roguery, boasting, lies, and sagacity."

A Cloud fresh out of law school, demented by Socratic questioning, has been assigned to justify the violations of signage law in our once fair but now blighted city. The violations are obvious to code enforcement officers as they pass by them and do nothing every day, but they are afraid to take the initiative, insisting that some village fool who happens to know the ordinances fill out a complaint form and thus risk almost certain retaliation from the lords of the land, who reason that since men made laws they can break them and make their own laws because they are men as well. A moratorium on enforcement has been declared, but enforcement officers are afraid to say by whom or why, and refer reporters to the public relations Cloud whose hazy answers standing the law on its head leave us dazed. If the city attorneys beholden to the Clouds had their way, their clients would have all rights and no duties, would enjoy sovereign impunity forevermore, never paying their debt to society.

Indeed, we recall Strepsiades' mission. He sought out Socrates to learn how to plead his way out of debt. He found Socrates suspended in a basket, and asked him what he was doing up there.

"I have to suspend my brain and mingle the subtle essence of my mind with this air, which is of the like nature, in order clearly to penetrate the things of heaven. I should have discovered nothing, had I remained on the ground to consider from below the things that are above; for the earth by its force attracts the sap of the mind to itself. It's just the same with the watercress."

"What? Does the mind attract the sap of the watercress? Ah! My dear little Socrates, come down to me! I have come to ask you for lessons."

"And for what lessons?" answered Socrates as he descended to earth.

"I want to learn how to speak. I have borrowed money, and my merciless creditors do not leave me a moment's peace; all my goods are at stake.

"And how was it you did not see that you were getting so much into debt?"

"My ruin has been the madness for horses, a most rapacious evil; but teach me one of your two methods of reasoning, the one whose object is not to repay anything, and, may the gods bear witness, that I am ready to pay any fee you may name."

Just Discourse and Unjust Discourse soon appear. Unjust Discourse argues that justice has no existence because Zeus was not put to death for putting his father in chains.

Ah! To this day theologians have insufficient theodicy to explain how a good god could suffer so much evil to be done to those creatures purportedly created in his image to decide what is good and evil. Surely there must then be two gods, as maintained by truly orthodox Zoroastrians, but for them good wins out in eons whereas here evil seems to prevail unto final dissolution.

How Not To Report Corruption In The City Of Miami Beach

I called the State Attorney's office 25 April 2012 and left a message for someone to call me regarding potential public corruption, saying the matter was urgent because people felt their lives were endangered.

I received a call back today 27 April from a person who identified herself as "the city." It took me awhile to determine which city - she meant the SAO office for Miami-Dade COUNTY.

I explained that I had documentary evidence that indicated an organization might be involved in a conspiracy to defraud the City of Miami Beach, and that I had someone who would be willing to speak to law enforcement to verify that evidence.

I was told to "go to the lobby" of the State Attorney's Office way over in Miami and ask someone there for directions!

I had to laugh, because I just came from the lobby of the Miami Beach Police Station, to which I was directed by the city's Internal Affairs.

I called IA at the recommendation of a top officer after I told him about the information I had, which might be useful if there was a case in it. An IA officer said IA had nothing to do with cases except where police officers were involved, which was what I had figured in the first place.

I wound up in the lobby of the South Beach police station, and eventually laid out a summary of what I had to a detective whom I had been waiting around for 15 minutes while he was chatting with what appeared to be businessmen.

I explained that I could not report on the matter because the source would be endangered, but that the source would be willing to come forward to law enforcement.

He was most interested in whether I was wearing a wire or not. I responded that I did not blame him for being paranoid given the awful news about the police department, news to which I believe the community was overreacting to since every large organization is bound to have a few miscreants.

In response he persisted, saying I did not answer his question about whether I was wearing a wire. Of course not, I said, to do so without telling him would be a felony - if I did not have a warrant. Good thing I knew the law, he said.

He said I might have something big, but that he was in property crimes, and that I should go to IA. He asked me whether the City knew about the conspiracy to defraud, and I said certainly so, that the conduct is widespread, but I was told little could be done because it is hard to prove people were committing crimes in these cases.

When I told him I had already contacted IA, but was referred to the switchboard and instructed to ask the operator whom I could talk with, he said that IA does indeed have someone who checks out my kind of evidence, where the crime might be if the City had done nothing, and then he hurried away from me dismissively - without even a good bye or nice to meet you or thank you.

The Tardy Publication of Laws

Who would know what the laws are if not published at a single public place as has been done since ancient times by civilized cities, states, and nations?

If the City of Miami Beach were a civilized municipality, non-emergency ordinances would not take effect until thirty days after they are codified and published in the Municode. That is not the case.

According City Clerk Rafael Granado, Esq., the City of Miami Beach only publishes its coded ordinances at Municode every three months. Until then, one must rely on hearsay as to what the law is on a certain subject, or go to the city's search engine, dubbed "the fishbowl," to fish around for the latest ordinance, hoping the right terms have been entered.

I encountered some confusion among restaurant managers who heard the news from various sources back in May that alcohol sales and consumption at sidewalk cafes would be prohibited after 2 A.M. A few owners and managers had heard nothing official about it. Not all the flyers handed to employees by code enforcement officers got to their bosses.

The flyers said sales on sidewalk cafes would be prohibited at 1:30 A.M., not 2 A.M. A trip to the fishbowl turned up a second reading of the proposed ordinance, giving the time as 2 A.M. I checked with Mr. Granado, and he supplied copies of signed ordinances related to the prohibition, with titles stating 2 A.M., but revisions had been made within the body of an ordinance, giving two times: 1:30 A.M. for the cessation of sales, 2:00 A.M. for consumption.

He also provided a copy of a defective announcement published in the paper, regarding only one of the three related ordinances, that a hearing would be held on the issue, showing the 2 A.M. title. He said the announcement constituted legal publication of the ordained prohibitions.

What? How can an announcement that an ordinance might be defeated or passed constitute publication of its passage? Why not publish the laws actually ordained? He did not answer, and neither did City Attorney Raul Aguila.

Even if published in the paper, does one have pore over all the papers and go to all the hearings to find out what laws are in effect? Since the price of the Miami Herald hit the ceiling, I rely on my readers to send me the few important local articles appearing in that paper.

I go to the Municode when I want to know what the municipal code is. If I want to read the ordinances and commission discussions thereupon, the ordinance numbers appear as footnotes in the pertinent Municode sections; then I know what ordinance numbers to enter in the fishbowl.

So August 2015 was upon us and we were still waiting for the ordinance to be codified. Unsworn code enforcement officers are sneaking around in the meantime, handing out $1,000 tickets on skimpy or no evidence of consumption at all, including a couple of beer bottles not cleared from a table at 2:06 A.M.

"Not to worry," one code officer said, "if you get Special Master Annette Cannon to hear your case. She has dismissed nine out of ten violations so far." Just how many tickets have been handed out is a secret guarded well by the computer unless you want to pay several hundred dollars to dig out a few public records.

Well, Ms. Cannon should dismiss them all. No scientific fiscal or economic impact study was conducted as required by the city's constitution before passing the ordinance, public notice in the paper did not conform to state law, and promulgation was defective.

Who knows exactly what the law is if it is not published in one place?

Pedestrians have complained about bicyclers on Lincoln Road for years. An ordinance was finally passed and published in the Municode prohibiting bicycling from 9 A.M. to 2 A.M., but it was not enforced, on the excuse that the computer was not programmed for citations, until a clamor was raised by the press.

The code also prohibits motorized vehicles, skateboarding and rollerblading at all hours. The signs posted, however, do not mention rollerblading. When that fact was presented to two cops lolling on their Segways in a shady doorway one hot day, they said rollerblading was definitely allowed at all hours on Lincoln Road. Nonetheless, the prohibition was published in the Municode. Does that mean that there must be signs for the prohibition to be valid? Rollerbladers think so, and they may be right—ask a lawyer.

As for residents still riding bikes on Lincoln Road, they bravely say, when politely reminded by pedestrians of the law, "I don't care," or "F**k you!" They cower and lie, however, when confronted by a cop.

I encountered a police officer working the boardwalk along the beach, and pointed out two rollerbladers who had almost run over a lady in front of Beach Patrol officers who were coming out of the central beach station, saw what happened, and just kept going.

"Is rollerblading allowed here?"

He was not sure, he thought so, but maybe not, for there had been changes, so he would have to examine some printouts when he had time. Well, he might use his cell to look in the fishbowl for new ordinances as they might not be in the code for three months depending on where we are in the cycle.

"I was taught never to believe what people say about the law," I said, "including lawyers and policemen, until I look at the law itself, but the municipal law is not so easy to get to on the beach. Laws are being made every month. I supposed I have broken several today without knowing it."

Police officers certainly know that theft and murder, for example, are always illegal. Lifestyle laws, however, often change.

Everyone should have immediate and easy access to the laws in one place. We no longer have to go to the forum to examine the law. We have the Internet, and the Municode, where all laws should be published in order to be effective, and not until then.

The Disabled Shopping Cart's Service Dog

The new Trader Joe's in South Miami Beach spawned animated controversy on Facebook in 2019 over a colorful blackboard sign posted at its entrance, to the effect that only dogs trained and certified according to the American Disability Act would be allowed in the store.

That is to say, leave your pets and comfort or therapy dogs at home. Or tie them up outside the store, where they might be stolen, because Trader Joe's, unlike some dog-friendly operations that wish to attract animal-loving customers, has no outside space devoted to a caretaker with animal refreshments.

"Hallelujah!" exclaimed a devout woman who stopped and studied the sign as others traipsed by with dogs. It was not long before a gentleman posted his objection to the disobedience, in the form of an unnecessary nuisance dogging Trader Joe's. His post was headed by a photograph of the sign and a shopper stepping over a dog on a leash, extended far beyond the front of a shopping cart bearing a child and pushed by its mother, neither of whom were paying any attention to what was obviously their pet sniffing traces of some dog that had previously passed by. The gentleman apologetically worried that he would be hooted off the platform for his revelation because many South Beach residents love dogs for their unconditional love and hate legal conditions to the public expression of that love.

Quite to the contrary: other customers, both able and disabled, and including dog owners, are accustomed to doggedly complaining about the doggone misbehavior of dogs in food establishments: dogs running loose; long leashes blocking passages; dogs defecating in aisles and in shopping carts; dogs urinating on the bottom shelf; dogs barking; dog fights; and pet dogs distracting legitimate service dogs;—not to mention their fear of contamination by communicable diseases because irresponsible people who care less for their dogs than themselves do not attend to their hygiene.

And they should complain. Everybody knows that service dogs trained to assist a person with a disability are generally allowed by the ADA inside food establishments where food is not being prepared, but other animals are prohibited by the FDA whether they appear to be a nuisance or not. Service dogs creating an intolerable nuisance or a risk or threat to the health or safety of people inside the establishment must be removed.

For instance, if the dog in the picture were a service dog, someone might trip over the unnecessarily extended leash. The manager has a legal right to caution the customer to heel the dog or leave the premises.

The customer might object, however, that her child is allergic to certain allergens found on floors, up to a distance of twelve feet around the child, and that she had trained this dog herself to sniff them out and bark. Since she is not required by law to provide any certification of the disability or training, the manager has a problem. If she is lying, she is subject to criminal misdemeanor penalties. I doubt if the chief of police would have his officers conduct a thorough investigation and arrest her even though millions of people would applaud him if he did, but I have queried the chief for his comment, and I shall ask for a record of the number of arrests, if any, over the last few years.

I myself noticed a dog inside Trader Joe's, tied to an unattended shopping cart smack dab in the middle of the floor behind the aisles. The poor dog was scratching frantically at its fleas. I stepped away lest my hairy legs be infested.

"This must be the blind shopping cart's guide dog," I remarked to myself.

The unkempt, limp-wristed owner showed up with arms laden with various food gimmicks from several aisles. He noticed me looking at his afflicted dog, and glared at me as if knowing he had been caught doing something wrong, then shrugged his shoulders and sashayed off to collect more goods without cart and dog. He was apparently mentally disabled, apparently unable to keep his undercover service dog healthy and close beside him while shopping. I felt sorry for the dog and its owner, and especially for the suffering dog and anyone contaminated by it. Dogs have a reputation for being "dirty."

True, the risk of contamination at home or in public places is rather low if they are kept clean. The dear dogs need oils in their skin, so they should not be washed too often unless they get into mud; they should be vaccinated against communicable diseases, and subjected to a monthly parasite prevention program. Keeping dogs is a big responsibility for which people need to be trained—no doubt dog keepers would howl protest if they were required to pass a dog care course and be licensed.

I was somewhat familiar with the service dog subject from my experience at the Publix Super Market on Fifth and Alton some time ago, two weeks after I observed a fight between three dogs in an aisle at the nearby Whole Foods—fortunately, none of the dogs were killed, as was the unfortunate dog in the infamous dog fight at a Petco store.

The Publix was chock full of dogs until complaints were filed with authorities who did their best to hound management into compliance. Again, the Food and Drug Act generally bans animals from food establishments, but the American Disability Act provides a public accommodation exception for service dogs, which are by definition trained to assist a person with one or more disabilities. A partially blind public official shopping at Publix proudly showed me the certification patch on the vest of his service dog. He told me it can cost upwards of $30,000 to specially train some service dogs. On the other hand, so-called service dog vests can be purchased online for a few dollars.

Security guards at the Publix were observed stopping people with dogs for a while, asking them what disability their dogs were trained to help with, but all sorts of dogs have recently returned in force. I saw a little old lady with three cute dogs standing near the security guard regularly posted during the evening shift. A Publix employee whom I addressed on the subject told me employees look the other way when they see dogs, like this woman with three dogs, because she could claim some special disability requiring her to have three dogs.

"Maybe it's because bad things come in threes," I said, "or perhaps Catholics are required to have three service dogs for religious reasons, the Trinity, no less."

She said Publix settled a complaint against the company brought by a woman who was carrying a dog that was frantically barking and barking. She was asked to leave the store. The woman allegedly filed a complaint, claiming that she need the barking sound to give her a sonic bearing to navigate the aisles.

To return to Trader Joe's, a professedly disabled gentleman, seemingly provoked by the image of its sign posted on Facebook, complained about it, and then triumphantly barked:

"This illegal and discriminatory sign was finally taken down by the regional manager as of noon HOORAY!"

"The sign itself is not illegal or discriminatory," I rejoined, knowing that he would probably demur. "It was an innocent mistake. Signs do not discriminate. Only persons do."

The self-righteous gentleman was adamant. He commanded me, as if I were his dog, to never comment on things I know nothing about.

I am a dog spelled backwards as far as I am concerned, and both dog and god service humankind as guides. We may love the dog even more than the good old god we are admonished to love or else. Apparently the dog, who loves humans unconditionally, which happens to be a most wonderful survival stratagem, is replacing Jesus: an expert in canine cognition, the nature of which, like human cognition, remains a mystery, has written a book: *Dog is Love.*

Unlike the new god of love or the terrifying old god whose role our disabled adversary adopted, I find it convenient to be reasonable and to engage the world dialectically, if not logically, since the best logicians know that dialectics is a sort of illogical, running compromise that tends to rationalize evolving prejudices. The gentleman who is disabled by what he knows would stifle dissent, but without reasonable opposition, the wheel of civilization will not progress to its inevitable collapse and the rise of something hopefully better. An omnipotent god does not have to reason, but my ego is made in a faulty image of absolute power.

I have learned so much from free speech that I cannot stop talking; that is my disability, one that caused my application for a job with the Outfit to be personally rejected by Sam Giancana: "Kid, you talk too much," he said, and referred me to an employment agency in the Loop. Wherefore I speak up, and now this man would give me absolutely no quarter, insisting that everyone has to be as expert as he is on the subject in order to speak to it. He said not a word about the position of the dog in the picture posted, why people should have to step over it, and that the law provides owners with a right to remove service dogs that threaten the safety of their customers.

So, for the sake of argument, I checked out the ADA again, and also the pertinent pronouncements of the Department of Justice regulating the Act. There is no such thing as ADA trained and certified. People can train their dogs themselves if they like and buy cheap vests and certificates, or they can have their dogs trained and tested by numerous businesses happy to do so for a fee, certificate included. In fact, it is improper for establishments to require any physical evidence whatsoever from any person that their dog is a service dog. They may ask if the dog is a service dog, and, if the answer is yes, inquire into what disability is it trained to help with. It is illegal to discourage disabled people from using public accommodations.

So the man who appointed himself to represent the disabled community was correct when he insisted that the sign itself was illegal because it discouraged disabled people with service dogs from entering the public store. Still, I insisted that it was only discriminatory to the extent that management intended to abide by health and sanitation regulations, discriminating against persons whose dogs were not service dogs. The person drafting the sign had no intention of discriminating against disabled people. The sign was taken down and another one put up banning pets including comfort animals that are not service dogs.

I confessed what I had discovered as a result of his criticism of my free speech, and offered my hand in Facebook friendship. It occurred to me that everyone should have a disabled friend, and then they would have a plethora of friends if disabled people are a minority. The last time I looked, he had less than a handful of Facebook friends, while I, on the other hand, have nearly 500 and aspire to obtain the 5,000 maximum allowed by Facebook, in the name of the "community," as if we had voted on the rule. He declined the friendship on the grounds that Facebook friendship is meaningless or worthless. I am sure Facebook would definitely disagree all the way to the bank. I happen to find it spiritually rewarding, perhaps addictive.

"How do you know if a dog is a fake service dog?" I asked. "You really don't know if there is no certification required. How do you know the person with the dog is disabled? You may not be able to tell. Blindness has been successful faked by con artists. I would make sure the Moron Service Dog Act would require certification of both the animal and the disabled person. The certificate would bear the photo of both the animal and the disabled person."

Naturally any compromise was out of the question; anyone who proposes a resolution, according to him, must be a Nazi. Friendly discourse is rejected because Either/Or is irreconcilable. Therefore I am presumably a Nazi persecuting Jews. And that despite my hypothetical genetic association with the rebellious Habiru tribes, and my descent, according to my messianic father, from Jeremiah, the dissident real estate dealer.

"Yes, let's create a new certification that creates an unjust process for the disabled," he said on behalf of the disabled community. "A certification whose only existence is to address the insecurities of the non-disabled. I really love the idea of forcing the disabled to self-identify to make you feel better. You should force us to get tattoos like Hitler made the Jews. Then you will easily be able to identify us and you can food shop in peace. Problem solved...."I was not surprised by his effrontery, for I had taken some time to examine my critic's self-portrait throughout the blog, and was convinced he is disabled. Disabled people have good reason to complain. They were killed and eaten, or left in the bush or desert to die by primitive peoples. I suppose I could have really gotten his goat by recommending ovens be set up for service dog scofflaws, or, to be merciful, branding on the forehead, or amputation of a hand.

As a matter of fact, there are many certifiably disabled people who believe a better compromise could be had, that a definite line could be drawn on this issue other than anarchic "justice is to each his own." It was also Socrates who repeated the primordial myth that an adult without a sense of justice should be executed or banished. Accusing people of being Hitlers or Nazis for simply wanting justice is unjust, just another form of intolerance. What is the difference between a Nazi and a Jew when it is reduced to fading symbols once clearly emblazoned on disabled tanks that now sit rusting on devastated grounds? The walls, the laws, are rubble; the canines are dining on human flesh as a few old survivors sit and rend their garments.

I refused to shut up—I am obstinate when I am ordered to shut up for no good reason. This little teapot tempest helped me understand why people may think dogs are morally superior to human beings; that is, if unconditional love is ethical, a notion a man might disagree with if his wife expects him to be her dog, and vice versa.

I once caught a neighbor of mine, a Miami Beach drug dealer who liked to get crazy on crack, beating his huge St. Bernard with a broken off broom stick. The poor dog just cringed and whined, looking lovingly into his owner's eyes. I had warned the man that I did not care what he did as long as he did not disturb my peace. Now he had done just that. He heard me talking to the police. He disguised himself, threw the broom stick in the dumpster, and fled down the alley, leaving the dog on his doorstep. Fortunately for the dog, his beloved master succumbed to HIV soon thereafter, and the dog now has a loving master and a son.

Dogs do not know the difference between a service dog and an emotional support or therapy dog, nor do they have idea why only service dogs are welcome in grocery stores, restaurants and other food establishments. But able people who indiscriminately violate the ban presumably know the reason very well. Although humans have good reason to love dogs more than each other, and vice versa, dogs have been deemed "dirty" or unsanitary since ancient times. Wherefore the current ban, which is more or less ritualistic or scientific. Mind you that we know humans who are dirtier than dogs and people who do not keep their dogs clean.

PLEASE BE COURTEOUS
TO YOUR MUSLIM
NEIGHBOURS

MANY MUSLIMS LIVE IN THIS AREA AND DOGS
ARE CONSIDERED FILTHY IN ISLAM. PLEASE
KEEP YOUR DOGS ON A LEASH AND AWAY
FROM THE MUSLIMS WHO LIVE IN THIS
COMMUNITY.

The total ban has been ritually extended to the home by numerous Muslims, some of whom want dogs banned from all public spaces for religious reasons, according to Sputnik, a Russian propaganda outlet reporting on the "colonization" of Europe by Muslim immigrants. Islamists insist keeping dogs as pets is animal abuse and against Muslim law. Fanatics call for a boycotting jihad against grocery stores who allow any dogs at all in stores, and some have allegedly gone go so far as to poison dogs.

On the other hand, the dog has been recognized by Muslims as an indispensable guide and as pets. They claim there is no original hadith against having dogs in the home despite the "fabrications" to the contrary. The Quran assured cave dwellers who kept hunting dogs in their abodes that their dogs would guide them to food. Dogs protected their flocks from predators and thieves in the country and ate the garbage in cities.

Dogs are naturally friendly to all sorts of animals. They relish meat including human corpses. Eventually dogs were associated with diseases breaking out near garbage dumps and cemeteries. Other sanitation means were employed; dogs were deemed useless and subjected to eradication. Other cultures ate the dogs who ate the garbage. Today an estimated 30 million dogs, stolen pets and dogs from dog farms, are consumed in Asia. My father, after being kept awake all night by a barking dog chained to a stake, and the failure of the police to do anything about it, recommended that dogs be canned and sent to Asia to feed starving people. Perhaps he should have recommended that the dog's owner and the police chief also be butchered and canned. After all, humans eat meat and are animals themselves.

In any event, it pays to be man's best friend despite an occasional beating—some women would agree. The dog has made a big comeback of late, so much so that it behooves competing politicians and newscasters to be seen with dogs, the only true friends they may have in their struggle for survival.

Domesticated animals do provide an objective connection to man's own animal nature, a nature that instinctively loves itself and anyone who will feed it regardless of its disabilities. There are several kinds of disability, blindness being the most obvious one. I hate to be dogmatic, but Section 413.08 of Florida Statutes, reflecting federal law, states that a service animal must be trained. Documentation is not a precondition. An out of control animal may be removed, if it is not housebroken, or poses a threat to the safety or health of others. It is a crime to interfere with the rights of a disabled person or a trainer. It is a misdemeanor to misrepresent oneself as qualified to use service animals. Animals must be on a leash unless that would interfere with its task. An individual with a disability has the right to be accompanied by a service animal in all areas of a public accommodation that the public or customers are normally permitted to occupy. An individual with a disability means a person who has a physical or mental impairment that substantially limits one of more major life activities of the individual, such as caring for oneself, performing manual tasks, walking, seeing, hearing, speaking, breathing, learning, and working.

A mental or psychological disorder must meet one of the diagnostic categories specified in the most recent edition of the *Diagnostic and Statistical Manual of Mental Disorders* published by the American Psychiatric Association, such as an intellectual or developmental disability, organic brain syndrome, traumatic brain injury, post-traumatic stress disorder, or an emotional or mental illness. A service animal is an animal trained to do work or perform tasks for an individual with a disability, including a physical, sensory, psychiatric, intellectual, or other mental disability, and may include, but are not limited to, guiding an individual who is visually impaired or blind, alerting an individual who is deaf or blind or hard of hearing, pulling a wheelchair, assisting with mobility or balance, alerting and protecting an individual who is having a seizure, retrieving objects, alerting an individual to the presence of allergens, providing physical support and assistance with balance and stability to an individual with a mobility disability, helping a person with a psychiatric or neurological disability by preventing impulsive or destructive behaviors, reminding an individual with mental illness to take prescribed medications, calming an individual with post-traumatic stress disorder including anxiety attack, or doing other specific work or performing other special tasks. And that is not all—hire a lawyer.

A law is a sort of line that walls off unacceptable behavior. If we carefully examine the existing laws and regulations on this subject, we get the impression that the wall has been lost in the definition, or that hordes of violators are climbing over it with impunity. Smart scofflaws know the law and lie accordingly. People unwilling to lie simply leave and come back later. A law unenforced is not a law.

Why, anyone might be disabled according to the laws and regulations on the books. The Diagnostic and Statistical Manual of Mental Disorders and its precedents employed as a guide to determine mental disability has long been criticized by the anti-psychiatry movement as unscientific for its comparison of arbitrary patterns of superficial behavior with a presumption of normality, as an unreliable tool with categories that no two objective professionals can agree on, and an expanding number of descriptive categories that by interpretation might ultimately include everyone since the ideal of "normality" does not really exist. At one time, homosexuals might have needed a specially trained service dog to straighten them out and keep them from cruising meat markets

Indeed, humankind by nature is disabled. Eminent legal scholar Edmond Cahn wrote, in a chapter entitled 'Partial Disability', or disabilities preceding death, in *The Moral Decision*, a book that used to be required reading for first year law students, that everybody is disabled in a certain sense:

"If we are to evaluate disability reasonably and soberly, I think we must begin by directing our gaze not on the disabled but on the remainder of society—on those who are usually considered 'able.' What do we see then? That every one of the so-called 'able' is in some respect or other in some degree disabled. We are all partially disabled, because mental and physical perfection—like all other professions—is only for diagrams. The old among us suffer from a thousand elements and degenerations, slow reflexes, insecure gaits, weak perceptions. The young, even the healthiest so then, carry the ordained disabilities of youth, which include heedlessness, impetuosity, absorption and passionate musings, and the irrational compulsion to take risks merely for the sake of thrills. Large numbers of the youth in every country are blighted with mental, nervous, or organic defects and disorders which may pass unnoticed until a military conscription system provides an occasion for medical examinations on a mass scale. Physical competence is all too often canceled by mental or nervous handicaps, and the minority of young men who happened to excel in both mind body will provide a substantial part of the casualty lists in periods of wars. There we usually are not aware of it, every street and avenue has among its pedestrians a full a share of alcoholics, drug addicts, psychotics, congenital morons—not to mention the individuals of in perfect eyesight who have to put on glasses to write a book or read one. And whenever a person's attention chances to flag for a moment, the finest natural endowments can become entirely useless to him; at any street crossing, alert and cautious valetudinarians may survive where athletic but inattentive youths will be struck and killed. Finally, we must allow for the remorseless caprice of chance, would sooner or later surprises and disables all."

He concluded that the progress of society depends on the intelligent accommodation and utilization of all its resources so as to mitigate the impact of the various disabilities of its members on everyone. To accomplish that end, we have a moral obligation to make sure that some obvious notice is given by the disabled to everyone else to avoid imposing guilt on them for any harms that might result from the failure of the disabled to give such notice.

In Cahn's example, a partially blind man who navigated a familiar area by vague outlines of things, tripped over excavated soil, fell into a trench, and was injured. The lower court gave him $500 for damages, but the superior court reversed on the grounds that he did not have a cane with him, which would be notice to the public court that he had taken reasonable steps to protect himself, so his own negligence probably contributed to his injury.

In our case, sympathetic legislators and regulators have disposed of the moral requirement so that no notice must be given by the disabled, thereby endangering the able public because everyone with a dog may enter with impunity. There is no line drawn in the sand or barrier at the door, and everyone is afraid to draw one because everyone may be disabled somehow, and they may be hooted down for objecting to non-service dogs because people love dogs more than each other and the law. Wherefore there is no enforceable law, and scofflaws proliferate to the harm not only of the disabled but the able as well as the merchants who serve them. Sadly, all too many people are blind to the injustice done by minorities to sympathetic majorities.

Again, a law unenforced is no law. The law banning dogs other than service dogs from public accommodations should be repealed or amended to require definite notice in the form of visible ADA approved certification of the disability of the person and training of the service dog. The universal disability license should include a photograph of the disabled person and his or her service animal. In any event, everyone is called upon to assist disabled persons in need of friends.

Signs of Respect on Lincoln Road

The dirt is in the details. I have little respect for soldiers and police officers who do not keep their boots and shoes shined, and none at all for property owners and their agents who do not abide by the signage and window-covering ordinances for their vacant shops.

Not only do negligent landlords and their realtors have little respect for the public, they have no self-respect, and it is a wonder why anyone would do business with them knowing that scofflaws who do not care about the conspicuous violations are likely selling or renting premises with hidden defects as well, probably gone unnoticed or ignored by building inspectors.

Michael Comras of The Comras Company has won my First Prize 2019 for making sure that little details, such as getting a permit for signs on properties he is developing or renting, are taken care of. When someone is looking for space on the beach, I refer them to him, and say, "He has a lot of quality space all over town, and he abides by the signage law, which is a good sign that the property is in good order."

Of course just getting a permit for each sign and covering up the windows of vacant shops is the bare minimum a law-abiding property owner and realtor can do. Still, although it is said that a book should not be judged by its cover, an attractive cover will at least get a prospect to look inside. So I was a little disappointed when I revisited Lincoln Road to see that Comras, who teamed up some time ago with one of the richest billionaires in the world to pick up a big section of the popular mall, had used brown wrapping paper to cover the windows of vacancies.

It was not that long ago that Lincoln Road in terms of signage and window coverings was in deplorable state. One of the worst offenders was Stephen Bittel of Terranova, another huge investor in Lincoln Road, and head of the state Democratic Party as well until he resigned over an inappropriate behavior accusation. He was pushing for an exorbitant $400 a square foot yet he would not buy a $25 sign permit and put something nice in the windows of his offerings.

Lo and Behold, after numerous complaints to the city's code enforcement department, I noticed a sea change on Lincoln Road. Handsome and even beautiful window coverings appeared in the vacant shops. The code now requires the specifications to be approved by a committee. But the real estate magnates including Bittel have gone far beyond the minimum on Lincoln Road.

The bare minimum seems to be the brown wrapping paper. It can be seen slapped haphazardly into the windows of many vacant shops along Washington Avenue. It has so trashed the look of the drag that the code enforcement department has mounted an expensive, dragged out campaign to correct it. Some owners are using the city's paper, printed with a lifeguard station and sunbather. Maybe it is better than the wrapping paper, but residents have made an ethnic joke of it, which I will not repeat because it is unfair to Poland.

Do not be deceived, much of the vacant Washington Avenue property is owned by wealthy cheapskates and carpetbagger developers with money to burn. Even Jared Kushner is said to be in the mix. They obviously could care less about the neighborhood in their pursuit of capital gains for the few.

Maybe Comras will put something nice in the windows of his Lincoln Road offerings, like the one under Art Center/South Florida. I spoke to a British artist inside the art center about the brown window coverings. He said artists would probably be glad to draw something on the paper, free of charge, to advertise themselves, and the paper could be artistically constructed as well. The postmodern anti-art protest included printing attractive, repetitive designs on wallpaper.

It so happens that my favorite anti-art window covering is on Washington Road. It is in the vacant old shoe repair shop. It is Found Art now because I found it and took a picture.

My Favorite

Nice Coverings

Minuscule Thinking Adds Up To Corruption

In 2013 I pronounced foremost real estate firm Comras Company *The Worst Sign Offender in South Beach*. Since then it appears to be fully compliant. Scores of signs now bear permit decals as required by city ordinances.

Therefore I congratulate Comras Company for being a law abiding business despite the fact that other prominent firms do not bother with the permitting process because city officials, who can often be observed not attending to official business, simply do not proactively enforce city ordinances of several sorts.

Instead, the scofflaws prefer to wait for someone to complain at risk of retaliation. If the offender is prominent and prefers to persist with the violation, the citation will most likely be dismissed by the special magistrate, who is an arm of the city manager's office, or the violator will simply comply with the particular order to avoid the trouble and go on to commit multiple violations of the same sort in the future.

Business and city officials alike thought I was a rude man and worse for bringing signage violations to their attention, not to mention pointing out unlicensed contractors and architects.

I did so because I had good reason to believe that the signage violations were significant of widespread scofflawry and moral corruption, with a small percentage even being criminal.

Money is the most powerful god in Miami Beach, and if one has a lot of it much can be accomplished without complying with the law.

Georgie Echert, Assistant Finance Director of the city's Finance Department declared that permits cost a mere $15, and that the amount collected overall was "minuscule."

She declined to disclose how much money was collected, perhaps because the funds collected do not have a separate account, which makes it easier to bury things since it would cost people making public record requests thousands of dollars to cull them out

She was mistaken about the permit fee. It was not $15 but was $25.

All one had to do was fill out a simple form at the garage and hand over the money. No drawings were necessary to see if the signs were in compliance with the parameters laid out in the ordinance.

Georgie Echert and her immediate superior, Patricia Walker, the chief finance officer of the city, were forced to resign after the city said they manipulated paid vacation and sick time—they allegedly misused their leave time to improve the future payouts they would receive when they departed the city. It was rumored that the adjustments were a common practice hence appropriate.

We do not know how much money was involved. No doubt it was minuscule. Grains of sand, however, add up to a beach when diligently processed.

Comras Company, given its popularity, must have paid many hundreds of dollars in sign permit fees by now. I estimated its cost at over $2,000 per year. Perhaps its accountant will come up with an exact figure since private businesses have information systems capable of being queried on such details for an answer approaching the speed of light, while the city's Stone Age system has not been upgraded to medieval account coding.

All of my proposals to political insider City Manager Jimmy Morales and wealthy developer Mayor Philip Levine and his personal junta of commissioners to either rescind the law or to revise it so it would be easier to comply with and would require minimal enforcement were ignored, no doubt because my concern was minuscule compared to their grand development plans.

Pathetic Petty Politics Ala Miami Beach

Candidate Michael Grieco withdrew from the race for his commission seat citing family reasons. The Miami Herald spun the story to infer that he will be indicted momentarily for felonies carrying a prison sentences and large fines.

Political campaigns bring out the worst in people, and all we can do is hope the worst is not their true nature. Why, the slanders and libels are so rife that the courts, perhaps in accord with the doctrine of original sin, have virtually waived defamation law.

Of course, if a political campaign has plenty of money to waste, as did the campaign of Philip Levine, the wealthy media mogul and real estate developer now sitting as mayor in expectation of running for governor of Florida at the end of his term, the candidate's campaign may use the courts as a tool to bring a libel suit to shut people up, because even telling the truth will not protect the defendant from up to a quarter-million dollars to defend a political libel suit. Levine's campaign consultant even threatened to file a suit against a journalist for what she had not even said yet!

Mayor Philip Levine, Hilary Clinton's pal, spent over a million dollars of his personal fortune to seat himself and his bevy of commissioners, which rendered him a de facto, dictatorial strong mayor in a city with a weak-mayor, strong-city-manager charter.

One commissioner in the bevy was Michael Grieco, who served as the mayor's right-hand man until he "evolved" to bite the hand that once fed him, objecting to the egotistical mayor's dictatorial style as chairman of the commission, and taking him to task for some of his purportedly corrupt objectives.

As it is said in India, the disciple eats his guru and sits on his mat. Mr. Grieco, a former state prosecutor, filed to run for the mayor's seat. His main opponent was Dan Gelber, a former prosecutor, now known as "Pious Dan, the Tenth Commandment Candidate," because he used his political campaign email to blast a sermon on that last part of the Decalogue, which enjoins people from coveting things, a motive to which he identified as the very root of corrupt.

The oblique reference was to Mr. Grieco, who had just dared to refer to Mr. Gelber as "Dishonest Dan" for using a tactic called a "push poll" to imply that he, Mr. Grieco, is corrupt.

Mr. Grieco is very well liked, especially among the young people of Miami Beach, because he makes himself available to everyone and tries his best to address their main concerns. As a result he is spread very thin, and he is one of those people who might, when talking with you, turn around abruptly without a word and speed away to do something else. Moreover, he is somewhat thin-skinned, and he has a hyperactive temperament and may blow a gasket and use a few choice words when pressure mounts. He lives in my neighborhood so I often encountered him and have watched him get things done. His devotion to his family and community is most impressive. Yes, I have thought of punching him in the nose a couple of times, but he is in great condition, so I have sort of adopted him.

Mr. Gelber, on the other hand, was relatively unknown to locals until he attacked their champion, Mr. Grieco. The old-timers do remember his father, who was mayor decades ago, and under whose administration rents are said to have risen to keep up with his pro-development bias.

Politically oriented people know the son had run for state attorney general, where he harped on his experience prosecuting public corruption, and he cursed the influence of political action committees while enjoying the benefit of PACs himself, including even a Republican PAC, or so it was said of this Democrat who coveted the job.

He quickly made a name for himself in the mayor race with free publicity in the Miami Herald. He accused Mr. Grieco of having a relationship with a PAC to which some contributors were city vendors. That potential conflict of interest, of a sitting commissioner, is prohibited by recent amendment to the city campaign finance ordinance, which provides for a $500 fine and vendor disqualification. If bribery were involved, criminal penalties are provided for by state law.

At first he denied involvement with the PAC. The Gelber campaign funded a handwriting analysis to discover Mr. Grieco's hand on PAC documents. Well, said he, putting on his lawyer hat, I was just the lawyer for the PAC, and attorney-client privilege barred me from revealing that relationship with the PAC. Baloney, scoffed the lawyers.

Exactly what his relationship to the PAC was is as yet unknown. The matter was referred to Katherine Rundle's office, the local state attorney for whom Mr. Grieco once worked. Ms. Rundle has done a good job with cases prosecuted, yet she like other prosecutors enjoys a "prosecutorial discretion" that gives people cause to suspect her of selective enforcement due to political bias.

Quite frankly, Mr. Grieco's supporters, many of whom do not read the Miami Herald, a paper well known for its political spinning in favor of whosoever the editors think will win and to whom the paper needs access for "authoritative" or "real" news, could care less about the PAC. Those entities now attract unlimited contributions because the Supreme Court ruled the caps on spending unconstitutional infringements of speech.

PAC advertising money does not buy the office; it buys name recognition and advertises political platforms, including the usual anti-corruption plank, that are invariable broken after the elections.

A candidate whose campaign cannot raise, say, a quarter-million dollars directly in limited contributions, will not raise much PAC money. The current numbers indicate that an indirectly related PAC receives, on the average, about the same amount of money as the direct campaign. Today, for example, a U.S. Senate seat costs around $20 million, half of that PAC money. Furthermore, factors other than PAC advertising help determine elections; big money does not always win.

Now the scandal over Mr. Grieco's little PAC, if it is his baby, which remains to be seen, reminds of the scandal over his former sponsor's relationship to a "dirty filthy" PAC.

Mayor Levine, running for his second term, was apparently tired of spending his own money for his seat, hence was calling vendors and developers to contribute funds to a PAC headed by a commissioner sitting with him on the dais. That is what resulted in the new ordinance prohibiting such behavior, although most real estate developers were not included in the prohibition because they are the biggest source of campaign funds so their free speech is sacrosanct.

When I mentioned to an editor that these PACs are just paper tigers, he said that is true, but they "change public perception," and that sells papers.

This paper tiger clawed Mr. Grieco badly. He dropped his campaign for mayor, and is running instead as incumbent for his commission seat.

I do not believe that the PAC scandal alone caused him to switch horses in midstream. Neither he nor Mr. Gelber have responded to my questions as to whether a truce was called and a PACT made that would allow Mr. Gelber to take the mayor's seat virtually unopposed, and Mr. Grieco to retain his seat because he is more popular than Mark Samuelian, who said he is "thrilled" to have raised several hundred thousand dollars for it, apparently because he thinks dollars are votes.

By the way, commissioners are paid $6,000 per annum, and mayors are paid $10,000. Mayors under the weak mayor system have no veto power. They serve as the chairperson of the commission, communicate with the administration, and speak publicly for the city. The low pay fosters corruption and elitism, an issue to be taken up elsewhere.

Mr. Samuelian, who had spoken well of Mr. Grieco, was obviously shocked to suddenly have him as an opponent. He immediately raised a big, green, four-way street sign on Facebook:

"ETHICS - RESPECT - INTEGRITY – HONESTY: Just when we thought Michael Grieco couldn't be any more shameless, we just learned that he will be folding up his criminally-investigated mayoral campaign and joining the race for Miami Beach Commission, Group 2.You have to wonder, if even Grieco knows he has so disgraced himself that he is unelectable for mayor, why would he believe he deserves to be reelected to the city commission? A commission seat is not a consolation prize, nor a place for Grieco to rehabilitate his tattered reputation. Miami Beach deserves much better."

An infamous political harpy followed suit with multiple excremental postings in the comment boxes, but she did not manage to cover with guano numerous complaints of Mr. Samuelian's "Friends" that he had triumphantly stooped to publicly dishonor a man who had done much for the city.

At least Mr. Samuelian could have waited a day for the burial; rabbis have said that it is alright to hate an enemy but his defeat should not be celebrated at the moment of triumph.

But this was really no triumph. It was agreed that Mr. Samuelian was simply crapping his pants, having learned he would have a formidable opponent, and perhaps knowing that incumbents need far less money than the amount he is "thrilled" to have already in his coffers, and knowing well that Mr. Grieco has several hundred grand that his contributors will probably consent to be used for his run for commissioner instead of mayor.

To make matters better for Mr. Samuelian's better-than-thou campaign, Mr. Grieco was heard shouting rudely at his aide.

The aides of commissioners work for the mayor, and this mayor, a close friend of the Clintons, an amateur politician with an eye on the upcoming gubernatorial race, is extraordinarily vindictive. We do not know exactly what was said, but hearsay has it that Mr. Grieco wanted her to work on his campaign. If he did try to coerce her into doing so, that would be a misdemeanor. So that matter was also referred to the state attorney.

Suffice it to say that Mr. Samuelian has tried and convicted his opponent of the worst, and, of course, not because he covets power, but only because he would protect the public from his very opposite, and he should be elected because he so squeaky clean that he has a right to cast the first stone at this virtual devil.

Up to this juncture, Mr. Samuelian was indeed generally perceived as a good man. The only reservation I personally had was over his limp-towel handshake. I have advised him to reach out and get a firm positive grip on the community, to limit the negatives to factual reports, and to refrain from being a political scumbag. I was about to speak with him on that subject at the Tuesday Breakfast Meeting, but he was huddling intently with former mayor Matti Bower and former commission Michael Gongora, probably conferring on integrity maintenance.

But nobody coveting power listens to me in this town anyway because they know the Miami Herald will not publish my commentary—an executive editor said that is because I do not suit the publication's "market needs."

Now I am hearing from all sides, including people who love Mr. Samuelian's integrity and an editor who likes Mr. Grieco, that all has not been told about the candidates. In August, which happens to be this month, the worst sort of corruption will be revealed, or so it is said.

The vague insinuations give one cause to imagine all the candidates being criminally indicted, handcuffed, and led off to jail.

"Well, exactly what crimes have been committed?" I asked. "I will be glad to report the facts, although it is up to prosecutors to present them to judges and juries."

"Oh, all that is for law enforcement to hear, not you," is the response.

So much for the petty politics of a city that awaits the advent of the Good Man, aka the Messiah, or at least a gentleman politician.

Afterward: Michael Grieco dropped out of the race altogether after he was charged. He did not contest the charge under condition that his record be wiped clean on good behavior, which it was. Then he ran for state representative and won hands down. 'Pious Dan' Gelber rejoiced, was elected mayor, ran again unopposed, and in 2021 is expected to win due to his funding and his support by the Jewish community. The Florida Bar finally got involved upon someone's complaint and slapped Grieco on the wrist. Mark Samuelian is running again in 2021 for commission seat, unopposed because he had a friend expose his opponent and neighbor for apparently not being a qualified resident of the city.

Excremental Note Re Man Without Qualities

I must beg your pardon, ladies and gentlemen, for this note on our excremental culture is long overdue.

Few people read signs anymore except to disobey them unless they are punished for ignoring their warnings. For example, dogs run loose in South Pointe Park while their excrement piles up around the signs that warn dog owners that the dog leash and dog waste ordinances are strictly enforced. The Code Compliance officer parks his car in the middle of the violations, goofs off on his cell phone for an half-hour, then files a Dog Patrol Report, swearing that he saw 17 dogs on leashes and no violations. For reasons unknown, since he saw no violations, he also reported that he indoctrinated several visitors on the dog ordinances. Perhaps he felt it would have been proper to preach since it was Sunday.

His featherbedding had gone unnoticed by administrators busy feathering their beds. Little does he know that his misprision and mendacity is a sign that Spengler was right about the decline of our so-called civilization, and that doom is impending in South Florida as hurricane season approaches to cap off an extra-extra high water event.

This Sunday, after reading a chapter from Robert Musil's *The Man Without Qualities*, as is my custom when visiting South Pointe Park, I opined that a busybody association must be formed to reform our excremental culture.

The man without qualities, named Ulrich, did not hesitate to recommend that people organize associations based on their common interests. For example, there was the stamp collector who believed collecting stamps fostered friendship between nations and satisfied the aesthetic sense as well as desire for owning property of substantial commercial value. And there was a man who was inordinately fond of shorthand. He had already set himself up the great patriotic Ohl Shorthand System Association, which he wanted Ulrich to bring to the attention of Secretary Leinsdorf as a device far better than the established shorthand system. The Ohl System would surely save time and mental effort, and rid writing of asinine longhand, so-called because of its long-eared script.

However, while engaged in conversation with a government official named Count Leinsdorf, Ulrich protested that the tendency for people to form associations had become more than just busybodyness in the highly organized state, where, "With all its law and order, everyone still belongs to some band of highwaymen..."

But Count Leinsdorf confessed a weakness for associations, which were essential to the progress of the state, or at least to the politicians responsible for it. A statesman, he said, must attend to its parties, institutions, and so on, that is, to its associations, in order to set a nation on its feet so it could walk of its own accord. Therefore, not only democrats but aristocrats must be as nice as they can be to people who come to them for help with their causes whatever those causes might be.

"You see," he told Ulrich, "with these things you can never tell whether they are nonsense or not. But the point is, my dear fellow, something important regularly results from the sheer fact that one attaches importance to something.... We must be up-to-date, don't we? And when a great many people are in favor of something, one can be sure that something will come of it."

As for political associations, the Count knew that struggles for the realization of limited ideologies would do a great deal of damage to society-at-large, for an ideology represents the tooth and claw of a political beast striving to be king at best. And the Count obviously had in mind Kant's observation, that the only unconditional good or good without qualification is a good will, regardless of its hypothetical consequences. To have a good will is the indispensable condition to happiness, and, for that will to be good for all, one should act according to a universal law or categorical imperative; to wit: "Act only according to that maxim whereby you can at the same time will that it should become a universal law." At issue is that, if one does unto others as one would have done to himself, he must sacrifice goods that he wants for himself.

"You must bear in mind that no good has ever yet come of ideological politics. What we must go in for is practical politics.... Practical politics means not doing the very thing one would like to do. On the other hand, one can win people over by granting some of their minor wishes.... Everybody, of course, would like to make all the beautiful ideas come true. That goes without saying. And so one must not do the very thing one would like to do! Kant himself said so."

Musil aptly observed, elsewhere, that "it is only criminals who presume to damage other people nowadays without the aid of philosophy."

This discourse against idealism led me to Ortega y Gasset's 'The Theme of Our Times,' in What Is Philosophy, a copy of which I had on my tablet. "The ancient idealist," he said, "believed that ideals were the only reality. The facts of experience long with the spread of modern scientific education eventually destroyed faith in immutable ideals. People were stripped of mass delusions and left alone with themselves, alienated, much to their chagrin."

"Idealism has been a rough and tenacious march against the grain of life, an insistent pedagogue trying to make it quite clear to us that to live spontaneously was to suffer an error, an optical illusion.... Even the miser could not enjoy the pleasure of continuing to be a miser if he thought that the piece of gold was only the image of a piece of gold, that is, a counterfeit coin....

"Once we are convinced that the beloved woman is not what we think her to be, but only an image that we ourselves generously made, the catastrophe of disillusion overcomes us."

So what is the theme of our times? "The Modern Age is melancholic, and the whole of it is more or less romantic." Romantics turned away from the ancient, presumably objective ideals. They became self-absorbed, self-tormented, concerned with the "I", one's innermost being, until it became an I-god or god unto itself. But that subjective "I" must have an outer or objective world to be and act in.

But not to worry: "We are no longer, fortunately, under the reign of romanticism, which led on exaggeration and impropriety." You see, modern man, no matter how romantic he might be in terms of his thoughts and feelings about himself, would manipulate his environment scientifically for his own good. He is a practical, or pragmatic. He experiments methodically, and his practice is based on experience.

Still, whom are we in love with in this allegedly neoteric age if not ourselves? When we say we love someone or something, whom do we love most of all? Would it be the category-of-one, the individual, our essentially infantile, narcissistic selves?

Returning to *The Man Without Qualities*, I was delighted to read about the man who had taken to examining signs while on the tram or walking the streets, and counting the number of strokes in the block letters of signs.

The letter A had three strokes, for example, and M had four. After dividing total strokes by total letters, he discovered that the average number of strokes was two and a half. Of course there were variations from the average. He found that divisibility by three was a "wonderful and rare exception" so that the rest of the signs imparted a feeling of disharmony except for the group with letters made up of four strokes, such a M, E, and W, and those four-stroked signs caused a "quite particular happiness" in the observer.

Therefore he recommended that the Ministry of Health be induced to generally suppress the number of one-stroke letters like O, S, I and G, to raise the degree of happiness in the sign-reading population. Statistics had already revealed profound relations among things long before they were explained, he offered. His theory would be proved true by anyone who counted the letters as he did, and that would improve their ability at mental arithmetic and ameliorate the damage done by excessive bookish education.

Is South Beach Like South France?

Hello, Richard! Someone complained that South Beach in Florida has become trashy like the South of France, and I said I don't understand that because I thought South of France was really great when the women after the war started shaving their legs. But I just talked to Aliz, and she said the problem was not with the hairy legs but with hairy under arms, and then I remembered hearing that the girls there do not wear underarm deodorant. So please let me know if South France is like South Beach. Yours Truly, David

David: One of my favorite places in the world is Cannes, France. Cosmopolitan, cool, trendy and attracts [people from around the world. I have spent a lot of time there. I have been with more than a few different girls there (locals and tourists). I have rarely seen or been with a girl in Cannes who has hairy armpits. Just don't see that there. I love French girls. Cannes is not like South Beach at all. St Tropez is not like South Beach at all. Nice is not like South Beach at all. Monaco is not like South Beach at all. French Riviera way more sophisticated and cool than South Beach. Yours Truly, Richard

South Beach Cash

Two shady looking gentlemen were at counter of CVS this afternoon with what looked to be at least $100,000 in $100 bills. They wanted to exchange them for money orders. The store manager said, "The limit is $2,500. Since there are two of you, $5,000 can be exchanged." So they had to go to other stores. That reminds me of when I tried to buy something with $100 bills in Washington on the commercial edge of Georgetown, and the cashier called the manager and the manager called two guards to stand by to protect me. I was coming in from Alaska, where cash was often used back then to do business, and I had a lot of cash on me. I sure wish I had it now. I would spend it all, again, every last penny.

The Best of All Possible Condominium Projects

"The Monad Terrace project on South Beach demonstrates," I said to my interlocutor over ham sandwiches at Whole Foods, "that there is nothing without the only good cause, that cause being no less than the one and only god, hence Monad Terrace is the best of all possible condominiums in South Florida, by virtue of representing the Monad of monads, the One of ones."

"I thought you were an atheist," said he.

"That depends on definitions. If you reason from the effects, it is obvious they all have causes, and it stands to reason that those causes themselves must have a cause, the first cause, which of course has no cause itself, whatever you want to call it, and is the very cause-in-itself or uncaused cause about which nothing greater than itself can be conceived except Nothing because Nothing is perfect and permanent. That is, the Essence Absolute, Supreme Being absent existence. "

"That is absurd."

"There can be nothing more logical."

"There is no longer a street named Monad Terrace because the condominium replaced it and the buildings on both sides. Isn't that a shame?"

"That is for the best, especially for the lady destined to hold out for top dollar. The Terrace still is and forever will be in the Monad as intended in the first place although the person naming the street was unconscious of the fact that one day a developer would snap up the parcels, and the virtue of the name would be celebrated by Jean Nouvel, who actually thinks architecture as a language. "

"I hear he is some kind of mystic, influenced in his youth by Dumas' *The Hunchback of Notre Dame*, which was historical preservation propaganda when penned."

"Yes, it was. Dumas saw architecture as a language being supplanted by the printing press."

"Weird. Anyway, there must be better places to live than at Monad Terrace. Take the White House in Washington, for example, where the greatest of American presidents to date lives with the most beautiful of ladies, the best model females can have."

"Trump said himself it is a dump, my friend, and spends as little time there as possible, rattling around late at nights in the basement like Hamlet. But that is beside the point, which is that everyplace is the best place for everyone to be for the time being depending upon who they are although some places are relatively better than others from those perspectives, and here the Monad Terrace is the best of all possible condominiums. Each unit is a world within itself, for which no windows are needed because windows and everything apparently external is really within, and that is the best of all possible worlds."

"Something will go wrong, defects will be found, and doom for Miami Beach is nigh for its sins."

"My friend," said I, "there is no good without attendant evil, no gods without devils. Evil is the cause of good and vice versa, while the cause of those causes is ultimately good otherwise the universe would collapse into chaos or absolute evil forthwith. You must consider the whole context, that some things and events are ostensibly bad for the betterment of the rest, hence bad is also good.

"Huh?"

"The bottom line is, you do have a choice when everything but that choice is preordained. Do you want to suffer miserably? No? Then suffer joyfully if you must suffer. Love life no matter what it brings. That much is up to you."

"This ham is excellent," said he, "I'm glad I'm not orthodox."

"The issue with swine was the roundworm Trichinella. Furthermore, swine needs a lot of water. Swine were created to be eaten by man every day and to furnish him with organs to implant because a man is almost a pig, or a hog if over two-hundred pounds, and diseases were created to employ doctors, just as I was given bad teeth to help support my dentist across the street. Arid deserts in part exist to save swine from being eaten by Orthodox Jews and Muslims so others can enjoy them."

"Good grief, you sound like Voltaire's Master Pangloss!"

"Pangloss is my preceptor and I his Candide, and here I am, finally, after all my travails, in the best of all possible beach towns if only I get to stay for a while in a Monad Terrace apartment and be recognized as one of the greatest authors Miami Beach ever knew. This is not El Dorado as some adventurers thought, for that is in the Maracaibo area of Venezuela, but everyone will at least secretly admit that things do not go so badly here, for otherwise they would move to Venezuela forthwith."

Grand Jorge Gonzalez South Pointe Pier Unveiled

The reconstructed pier at South Pointe, informally dubbed the Jorge Gonzalez South Pointe Pier in memory of the popular city manager who was forced into retirement by an opposition clique on a corruption pretext after 14 years of service, finally opened in 2014 with a great deal of fanfare by the new regime, happily taking credit for the completion of his project.

Mainstream newspapers trumpeted a grand opening celebration that, tellingly, did not really take place. Do not trust the so-called news when reports are based on press releases from a Clinton-backed regime that does not appreciate anything less than one-hundred percent appreciation of everything it does; or else it will blacklist reporters, refusing to provide official sources that the mainstream press relies on to hawk its rags.

Mayor Philip Levine, the wealthy real estate developer and travel publicity magnate who spent over a million dollars out of his own pocket to purchase a majority on the commission, and whose campaign brought frivolous defamation lawsuits against critical journalists, did not show up for the Sabbath event. He is ubiquitous nonetheless: he has lately been blanketing Facebook with advertisements consisting of pictures of himself with the Clintons and other superior public figures together with a statement that Miami Beach is a city that works for its people, but the people are not allowed to comment thereunder or to dislike the advertisements. Apparently he believes in credit by association with superior people although intelligent people deem that faith insulting to their intelligence.

The Sabbath scheduled for the grand opening was overcast, presaging stormy times ahead for the day and the censorious regime, which does deserve credit for expending hundreds of millions of taxpayer dollars on pumps that partially relieved city streets of troublesome flooding from the so-called "king tide" under October's full moon, an expenditure that Jorge Gonzalez felt would be a waste of money, to be rendered absurd by extreme high water events. Scientists are wondering what effect the pumping will have on the environment elsewhere. A Miami Herald reporter falsely reported one-hundred-percent dry streets.

Several faithful people including myself arrived at the pier thirty minutes prior to the scheduled opening ceremony. There were no art displays, giveaways, and refreshments available as advertised. A city public relations man slammed into me from behind as if on purpose, astonishing another city worker with whom I was chatting about government corruption as we waited for a ceremony that was not to occur. It was a beautifully gloomy and dreadful early evening. Lightning bolts were crashing around the bay with darkling Miami in the background. Several attendees hurried away as workers took a single little display tent down. A physical fitness expert who was there to promote her company hastened away disappointedly. I continued my productive chat with my confidential inside source, who was personally familiar with past corruption scandals, and who expressed concern with an ongoing grass boondoggle in the park involving a favorite city contractor and an allegedly negligent approach to remediation.

At the moment the ceremony was to take place, police officers arrived to inform us it had been canceled. Almost everyone had left, anyway, frightened by the spectacular lighting strikes. The downpour proceeded ten minutes later. I was duly soaked, but happy with the information I had obtained, and with the reconstructed pier itself, which is grand indeed.

Police Ticket Bicyclers on Ritzy Lincoln Road

City of Miami Beach Commissioner Michael Grieco responded August 2014 to our published concerns that the Miami Beach Police Department adopted a lenient, non-enforcement attitude toward violations of ordinances prohibiting bicycles on crowded Lincoln Road, where a resident complained to the Miami Mirror that a half-dozen bikes had passed her by, one cyclist actually pushing her aside, while a "nest" of police officers were mollycoddling violators by handing out warning flyers instead of ticketing violators.

On 11 June 2014, the city commission, responding to frequent complaints about the dangers to public safety bicycling presents on Lincoln Road, passed Ordinance 2014-3881 prohibiting bicycling on Lincoln Road between Washington Avenue and Alton Road between the hours 9:00 a.m. and 2:00 a.m., with fines ranging from $100 for the first offense to $1,000 for the fourth and subsequent offenses.

Bicyclist can dismount and walk their bikes, which has always been a common courtesy on crowded sidewalks throughout the civilized world, but so seldom observed with the decline of Western civilization that bicyclists have been stereotyped as sociopathic in several cities.

In response to our article, one David Granoff contacted Mayor Philip Levine, first congratulating him on his trip to Israel, and then complained that bikes, skateboarders, and rollerbladers speed along Lincoln Road while police do nothing—skateboarding and rollerblading on city sidewalks have been regulated since 1997.

"In New York City, they arrest and prosecute violators because people have been killed," Mr. Granoff wrote. "It is about time you address this and rectify this dangerous situation for good."

Mayor Levine, a public relations mogul and real estate developer, has scant executive authority under the city's strong city manager charter; however, the fact that he leads a so-called reform majority on the city commission provides him with clout similar to that of a strong mayor.

Commissioner Grieco, a criminal defense lawyer whose campaign for office was supported by the mayor and who often seems to serve as the mayor's right-hand man and the administration's apologist and publicist, and who does communicate with constituents and advance solutions to community problems, responded on 17 November to Mr. Granoff's pleading to the mayor, which had been copied to the commissioners:

"I have removed the other elected officials from this brief response due to the Sunshine Law. I am sitting at Books & Books as I write this (where I) just finished lunch with Chief (Dan) Oates. For every bicyclist we saw pedaling we saw six walking their bikes. I spoke with the staffs at multiple restaurants and they recognize the program working. Right now our goal is mitigation, as the signage and ordinance are brand new. I am very comfortable with rolling out the new prohibition with warnings and honey. That will end soon. We did not want to just hit people with tickets and scolding, especially locals, when they may be unaware of a relatively new rule. I promise you mitigation will progress to elimination soon, or as close as we can get. Thank you for your note. My colleagues and I recognize this issue as an important quality of life concern and are doing all we can without turning Lincoln road into a police state."

High ranking police sources informed the Miami Mirror that the reason ticketing had not begun since the law was passed nearly five months ago was not due to mollycoddling and honeying at all. The police department had simply been waiting for the city to integrate ticketing with the traffic court system. That issue had been resolved, so ticketing would proceed forthwith.

I visited Lincoln Road at 5:00 p.m. on 24 November. The Miami Mirror provides no budget for dining on Lincoln Road with VIPs, so after entering

Lincoln Road from Washington Avenue, I sat for a while on a curb near Pizza Rustica, and then walked back to Washington Avenue.

Warning signs were posted at every avenue transacting Lincoln Road. Plenty of bicycle racks were available on each block.

I observed twelve bicyclists, all of them apparently locals, over a period of thirty minutes. Only two were walking their bikes.

Two police officers confronted one rider in front of Pizza Rustica. He proceeded to plead with them, making excuses. Finally he dismounted. I wondered why they did not cite him.

After the officers continued along Lincoln Road, another bicyclist, who had observed the proceeding, pedaled around and around the area after the officers had left.

As I headed back to Washington Avenue, I saw one of the officers checking the identification of a bicyclist while writing a ticket. The other officer was dealing with a skateboarder.

The man being ticketed was complaining that he did not know about the law. The cop told him to tell that to the judge, at which point I recalled how a judge had told me long ago that ignorance of the law is no excuse, and how I had then warned everybody I encountered about the law and why I thought it was unfair. I had stopped payment on a check written to a dry cleaner because when I examined the clothes delivered to me, I discovered my best shirt had been destroyed. The judge was unsympathetic, and, wanting money to pay the fine, I had to wash police cars.

I queried several restaurant waiters and hostesses along the way since they are the ones dealing with the traffic along the walkways between the restaurants and the sidewalk cafes. Not one expressed any sympathy whatsoever for the bicyclists ticketed.

"They should ticket skateboarders and people riding bikes."

"Good for them. There are little kids and people eating here, and they could get hurt."

"I've always thought they should do something about the bicycles. They are very dangerous."

"The bicycle people have no respect, so maybe the tickets will teach them respect."

"People should follow the rules."

"They should be punished."

For the sake of balance, I am moved to mention a conversation I had the night before with a man at the Thirtieth Anniversary of Art Center South Florida. He was outraged that he had received a flyer from the police advising him that riding bicycles on Lincoln Road was prohibited.

"How dare they prohibit bicycling!" he ranted. "Whom can I contact on the commission about this?"

"Contact Commissioner Michael Grieco," I advised. "He is a defense attorney, is against a police state, and often posts news about police misconduct on his Facebook wall. He is the kind of friend you want to have if you get busted. He got into hot water with the Florida Bar when he was an assistant state attorney because he intervened for an arrested friend as if he were his defense counsel instead of a prosecutor. That was wrong, but I have mixed feelings about it. It raises philosophical issues about the antagonistic system."

Still, I am all for a police state when it comes to enforcing the prohibition of bicycling on Lincoln Road from 9 o'clock in the morning until 2 o'clock the next morning.

Bicyclist Killed By Trash Truck at South Pointe Park

I received a call on the afternoon of October 31, 2014, by a reader who had been following my stories about the careless and selective enforcement of traffic laws in South Beach including South Pointe Park. She said that Channel 10 News was reporting that a man had been killed around noon by a truck assigned to remove trash from a construction site in the park, and that the police were still on the scene. She sent me an image she had taken that day of a truck blocking a bicycle lane while she was out riding. She said that had happened several times during her ride, and that she was also confronted by hordes of motorized vehicles, Segways and Trikes operated by tour companies, despite the law against it, which is not enforced. She said she was tempted to accost the scofflaws, so I cautioned her not to do so lest she be assaulted since whatever respect some of them have, especially the males, is often limited to uniformed police officers.

The truck under which the bicycler reportedly died was being hauled away when I arrived at the scene. Two police officers, one of them a Motor Unit officer, were chatting at South Pointe Drive where Washington Avenue runs up to the park. As I crossed the street to speak with them, a driver did not yield the cross walk, passing a foot in front of me. Noting my alarm, the young scofflaw shouted that he had seen me so I should not worry.

I asked the officers about the accident, expressing my concern with the increase in traffic in South Beach and the negligent and selective enforcement of traffic laws against parking in bicycle lanes and failing to respect bicyclers on the road. I was assured me that this event was a "real accident," between a rubbish truck and a tourist riding a bicycle rented from Deco Bike, and not an incident the police or parking officers could be faulted for.

Deco Bike is the city's official bicycle renting and sharing program. It is a controversial program because the rental stations often take up scarce parking space by curbs near corners in high traffic areas, exposing people to hazards. When empty, the railings on the bike stations are the same color as the pavement during daytime. I remarked that the system is popular with tourists who are unfamiliar with our streets and the characteristic rudeness of drivers. Many tourists, I noted, have not ridden a bike for years as is made evident by their wobbling. One officer said he had tried one of the bikes, and found that the wobbling is caused by the instability of the front end of the bikes.

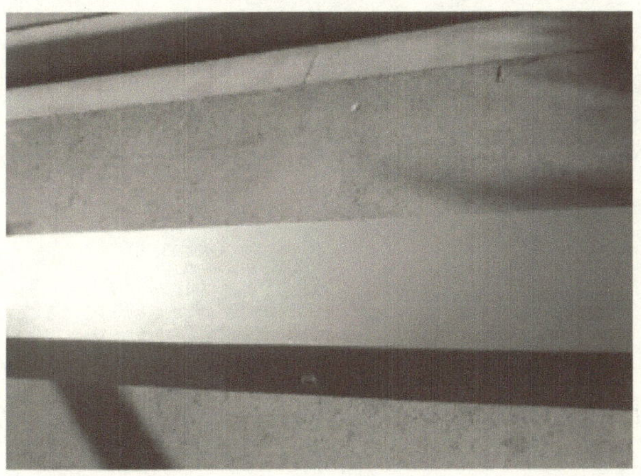

As I approached the Deco Bike stand near the entrance to the park, I was amazed to discover that the victim's mangled and bloody bike was stretched out on the sidewalk beside the Deco Bike stand, where it had apparently been abandoned by the accident investigators. It was not a Deco Bike. Beside it stood an undamaged bicycle of similar make and size and color, leaning against a pole, unsecured. At press time the identity of the unfortunate decedent was unknown, and it was unknown whether the undamaged bike belonged to a companion.

Plaza Construction Company Safety Officer Domingo Quintana was nearby, as if guarding the abandoned evidence. I asked if a tourist were involved. He pointed out the bicycle lock on the bike, and a bloody shoe trapped in the wreckage, and said it obviously did not belong to a tourist. When asked if Plaza Construction was involved, he said no, that the accident occurred when the truck was entering the park to remove rubbish from construction site there. He said he was in charge of safety at the two huge construction projects of Jorge Perez' The Related Group on the other side of South Pointe Drive, between Alton Road and Ocean Drive.

He said he had been on the scene since the accident had happened, to see if a construction worker was involved, and then simply to observe and report safety concerns. Safety officers with big construction companies are a sort of family, he explained, and consider safety around projects to be their general concern whether or not their companies are involved.

I said I had reported the concerns that a confidential source of mine, a public works officer, had expressed over the relationship of the city with the landscaper and plumber on the park project, dubbed a "grass-doggle" for the replacement of grass, and with the allegedly negligent method used to remediate the defects of brand new, water-fountain system. The contractor had hung large, unpermitted signs on the fences.

Quintana said the city's Code Compliance officers had forced the landscaping and plumbing contractor to take the illegal signs down. He said Compliance officers had also cited the Plaza Construction projects for unpermitted signs, giving them an ultimatum to take them down or go to special master court. A worker was nearly killed, he said, when removing the Plaza Construction signs from atop the cranes. The signs were affixed when the cranes were on the ground. I wondered if the signs included the license number as required by state law. I said that the signs should never have been mounted on the cranes in the first place and that I thought they were great advertising and should be the only contractor signs allowed as the others, especially the oversized MAREA real estate ads, were crappy. Still, the law is the law, I said. The fact that the law is violated on the face of a project gives me cause to suspect far more serious laws are being violated behind the signs.

Preferred city contractor's unpermitted sign

It is not absolutely certain the truck was to remove trash from this controversial site. A worker from Joe's restaurant nearby came over to say he was there when the accident happened. He did not actually see it, but he thought the bicyclist was trying to get away from the truck or out ahead of it as it was about to enter the park, and was run over. News reports said the driver got out of the truck screaming, and stayed on the scene as the man expired under the truck.

I asked Quintana what concerns he would report in respect to the bicycle accident. First of all, he said, the evidence had been abandoned. Secondly, the damaged bike was left stretched out on the public sidewalk right beside a large recession in the sidewalk, creating a hazard for pedestrians at night. Thirdly, the undamaged bike was not locked, and would probably be stolen within hours. Finally, he thought that the large pool of blood next to the bike station should have been cleaned up.

I e-texted Major Mark Causey of the Miami Beach Police Department and informed him of the situation. By coincidence, I received a call from another police officer on another matter immediately thereafter, so I told him about the situation, and he said it was definitely not right to leave evidence behind when someone had been killed, and that I should contact Major Causey. While I was speaking with him, police officers arrived and removed both bikes forthwith. Major Causey then responded to my e-text, stating that the evidence should not have been left on the scene, so it had been removed and secured at the police station.

I approached the Channel 4 and Channel 10 news crews to ascertain whether or not crime scene investigators had been on the scene inasmuch as Quintana said he did not actually see them examining the bicycle. Channel 4 had reported the man killed was a tourist. That could be if he was riding a friend's bike. The Channel 4 reporter was all ears. A cameraman took some tape of the bikes being removed. The Channel 10 reporter said the Channel 4 reporter did not know what was going on, and that she knew what was going on because she had watched crime scene investigators go over the scene thoroughly. She said that evidence is sometimes left behind on the scene by investigators for members of the family to pick up because the property belongs to the family. When I said that was improper police procedure, she said that is sometimes done and she could only say what she knew.

That is all I know at this time. No doubt the lawyers will want to consider all perspectives and accounts, which usually vary one from the other, even eyewitness accounts. For sure there was a bad accident. For sure we are saddened by the loss of the man who died. For sure everyone should be more careful and patient on the road. For sure everyone should wish family and friends well when parting, knowing that they might not see one another again.

COMMENTS:

On 11/1/14: Your article is much better than the networks. Channel 10 showed a picture of a bike being taken away by police saying "it is amazing how the victim's bike was not mangled. George

On 11/1/14: They would never have known if I had not told them and had them point the camera that way. I did not tell them there were two bikes, the mangled bike being the one the man was killed on. The older reporter was jealous of the pretty young reporter at the other channel. What a waste of money. Two media trucks and teams and a chopper for seven hours and they got story messed up looking and sounding good for TV. Cops said it was a "real accident." "The mangled blood bike was left behind on the sidewalk for the family," said the Channel 10 reporter. Lawyers may have a field day. David Arthur Walters

Bicycling On Lincoln Road

Bicycling on the sidewalks of Lincoln Road Mall has been prohibited for nearly a year. The ordinance has been actively enforced by the Miami Beach Police Department for six months in 2015 following complaints that police officers were merely handing out warnings. Commissioner Michael Grieco, a criminal defense attorney, had said that he was chatting at a Lincoln Road café with Dan Oates, the new police chief. Only half the bicyclists were violating the ordinance. The commissioner thought it was best to play nice with violators until everyone was familiar with the law.

Police sources said the problem with ticketing was the IT department had not yet programmed the computers for acceptance of that type of ticket. In any event, staff at sidewalk cafes said that the commissioner, a politician inclined to boost the new regime led by the new mayor no matter what it does or does not do, was almost blind as a bat because Lincoln Road was rife with violators as usual, much to the continuing consternation of pedestrians and businesses along the way.

The Miami Beach Police Department is good at responding to public clamors. Ticketing proceeded with a vengeance at the end of the year. That was a welcome gift for holiday visitors to the world-famous mall. The word got around locally that this particular minor ordinance, unlike several others, was being regularly enforced by the police department.

Advertising in the form of actual enforcement of the law was effective. As anyone who walks from one end of Lincoln Road can see, the number of bicyclers and skateboarders as well has radically diminished as a result of real enforcement. Pedestrians, bicyclers, and motorists would naturally like to witness this phenomenon on the city's streets.

Nonetheless, anyone will probably note a violation or two on every block of the mall, as I did on the afternoon of the Sixteenth of May.

I observed police officers sitting in their black-and-white vehicles that day as bicyclers passed by. That prompted a warning on their loudspeakers that bicycling was prohibited. That included a warning to a local bicyclist who had cursed at me, using the foulest of language and kept going after I politely warned him of the prohibition after he brushed me with his handlebars.

I saw no tickets written during my half-hour walk along the mall. Of course we all have our anecdotes. Statistics are always difficult to obtain from the police department, perhaps because it is damned for whatever numbers it comes up with: few arrests seem to mean cops are not doing their job, while many arrests are indicative of a crime wave.

Nevertheless, this article is an open invitation to Chief Dan Oates to provide for our publication a statistical report on Lincoln Road ticketing since the inception of enforcement (of course it was not provided).

Shoppers complained to a couple of local bicyclers who got in their way. I announced in a pleasant voice that bicycling is prohibited on the mall sidewalks. Again the response was insulting, and the deviants pedaled on their way.

"Locals know the law by now," I remarked to the shoppers. "They are scofflaws."

"They're sociopaths," said one passerby. "If a cop was around they would kiss ass."

"Excuse me, excuse me," pleaded a man on a bicycle behind me.

The man had a thick German accent. I recalled that Germans have a reputation for following rules, except, lately, the dog waste rule in Berlin, so I warned the gentleman that bicycling was prohibited on the mall sidewalks.

"I am sorry," he said, and hopped off his rented bike.

"You can walk your bike like that fellow," I advised, nodding at an obese exhibitionist parading along in a bikini bottom with head held high, "or you can secure your bike in a rack."

"I did not know."

"Notice the 'Pedestrian Friendly' signs on every corner. They are kind of small, and my vision is not so good so the lettering is difficult to read, but the icons are clear."

"Oh, I see. Is it okay to ride on other sidewalks?"

"Not if I had anything to do with it, but it is perfectly legal in most places, so do not worry about it if you do not see a sign against it."

I paused awhile to watch bicyclists playing around near the Regal Theatre end of the mall. Perhaps that end could be turned into a skateboard and bicycle park.

Constructive Criticism in South Pointe Park

Constructive Criticism is much better than a Positive Mental Attitude

Nothing is perfect, but someone is always worse off than we are here in South Beach. Marine Le Pen's dad told her to imagine being naked in the snow in the middle of a war if she believed she were in a bad situation. She might feel better if she immigrated to South Florida instead of getting her wallpaper stolen by immigrants in France. Thieves here have better things to steal.

Not much of an imagination is needed nowadays to see if someone else is worse off than we are and selfishly rejoice accordingly at our good fortune. All we have to do in South Beach, if we think we are having a bad time of it, is to watch the news, and then look around at the beautiful place we live in pending the Great Flood or the detonation of a nuclear bomb by terrorists.

My telephone alerted me this Sunday morning to some great video of dead and dismembered bodies amid the destruction of Mosul. There will be nothing left of the city after it is saved, and that nothing will indeed be perfect considering the horror that its existence is today. And then I looked around me as I took my morning walk to South Pointe Park. I was glad the news agency shared the apocalyptic revelation with me. My day was glorious by way of contrast.

Normally walking down the street is a nightmare for me because I notice all the violations of law, and wish I knew nothing of the ordinances so I could have a nice day. Now I almost had a positive mental attitude, but I cautioned myself not be like the PMA atheists and the Augustinians theists who would fain believe that there is no such thing as evil hence are themselves good for nothing. As most successful lawyers will tell you, complaints and counter-complaints are a very good thing, despite what Abraham Lincoln said about litigation; why, the very advance of civilization depends on them.

What is called for is not the complete suspension of criticism and a positive mental attitude, but a modicum of love of one's own kind and some constructive criticism. So I took my Sunday my stroll in the park with a critical but constructive attitude.

I recalled that John Rebar, Parks Director for the City of Miami Beach, did not respond to my requests for his scientific finding, if any, that the closure of South Park Pointe Park for re-landscaping by Superior Landscaping and Lawn Service was not a remediation boondoggle, as it was said to be by some of the affluent neighbors nearby, and by a city worker at the rained-out grand opening of the renovated pier. The remediation of what appeared to be good sod and grass was made shortly after former mayor Matti Bower and city manager Jorge Gonzalez completed the renovation of the park.

I neglected to inform him that another city employee, apparently a friend of former city manage Jorge Gonzalez, whom I had criticized for nonchalance, deliberately slammed into me at the pier in front of my confidential source. I was tempted to body slam him to the new pier, not only because he is a pipsqueak who calls himself "the fly on the wall," but because of the body-slamming technique I learned from a professional wrestler in a Minneapolis strip club after he picked me up and brought me down on a table, shattering it, but not badly hurting me.

Now I am no longer interested in whatever relationship Superior Landscaping might have had with the so-called reform regime of the city given recent events in France, including the statement of Marine Le Pen saying she loves immigrants, but they are stealing wallpaper, and a report I read on the Internet, saying the French public areas are covered by thick layer of dog excrement, and Americans had better not suggest that pooper-scoopers be handed out. I hear the sidewalks and curbs are just as bad in Berlin.

The most remarkable change for the better in South Pointe Park is that I saw only one dog without a leash during my Sunday visitation: a beautiful golden retriever owed by a wealthy gentleman who has sovereign immunity for violation of leash laws; and so do the park rangers who speak with him about it on rare occasions, and then leave him alone.

I like to watch the dog run around the park, onto the beach and back. The only I objection I have is the owner yelling, at the top of his lungs, "Go get the cat! Go get the cat!"

I understand his friend owns a pet business. No problem. Wild cats are not pets although lots of people try to feed them as the cats run and hide in the rocks and grasses. I would not be surprised if someone brings a real wildcat now that a man is bringing his pet pig to a beach park.

His shouting last Sunday interrupted my reading of J.J.C. Smart. It occurred to me, after considering the theory of mind-brain identity, that I actually knew I was simply having a neurological event, an occurrence that seemed to disprove the notion that my consciousness or attitude towards it was part of the process instead of independent to it.

Perception is not sensation, I reasoned, and perception of sensations depend on judgement, a decisive moral (mental) event which requires free will, so I can change my negative judgment of this man's shouting, "Go get the cat!", along with the multiple code violations I had noticed on the way to the park and in the park. I might even wrap about it in a hip hop vocal entitled, 'Go Get The Cat, Leave The Pig Alone.'

I just had to call my friend Aliz, who shares my opinions about the official negligence and scofflawry tolerated in South Beach, especially after faulty roadwork cause her to take a nasty spill from her bike on the way to the vitamin store, and then she was knocked off her bike by a negligent driver on Fifth Street, and then her bike was stolen in front of Macy's (probably saving her life); the police did not even care although Macy s had a video. Furthermore, she happens to love dogs, but not when they are running loose and crapping on the beach as police and code enforcement officers stand by chatting with each other.

"Aliz, I am in South Pointe Park. I just had a Kabala moment! I was studying mind-brain identity and my whole attitude has changed. I just flip-flopped like the President and had to call you. I see a half-dozen code violations right now, and they are beautiful! People are having a great time. They are free to read the signs and violate every rule!"

"I wish I had my bike," she said. "I would come over to watch the violations with you. You know, most people go to the park to see how lovely it is, but we go to see the violations.

"Yes, and they are lovely too!'

"I never thought of that. But you are right. They are beautiful now that I think of it. What would we do without them?"

"I shall call you latter. I want to tweet about this."

I whipped off a couple of tweets, and then I walked over to the hill and examined the new sod that is being laid down as per our conversation. I thought about what Mr. Rebar said, that he would not charge the trainer, who has been exercising forty or so people at a time on one side of the hill before he moved to the other side, for replacing the damaged sod, and I speculated on why he is not required to have a permit yet submitted insurance information, and the nature of his allegedly special relationship with the mayor and sponsors.

I mounted the hill. A man paused at the bottom to read the sign prohibiting bikes on the hill, and then he proceeded to bicycle up the hill with a baby in the front basket and a boy following him on another bike.

The hill was a bit crowded; an obese man with two small children were in the path, so I said, "Sir, please, as you can see from the sign, there is no bicycling up here," to which he uttered "Go **** yourself," and continued.

I said to the obese man, "A park ranger said he regretted having the evil thought that someone would get hurt up here so he would be authorized to crack down on the hill violations," to which the man shrugged shoulders and said, "So maybe people will learn the hard way when someone gets hurt."

That someone could have been his kids, but never mind, that did not happen, and it was such a beautiful day.

Well, I guess nobody has been hurt, so who cares? And even if someone did get hurt, one has to consider the cost-benefit ratio, and that might justify an injury or two, correct? Seeing people have fun in the park like this is very pleasant, anyway. The violations are actually the beautiful part.

And then I saw two kids racing around below on self-powered "toy" vehicles; one on an ATV, the other on a scooter. A group of bicyclers came along, creating a bit of a traffic jam, and one of the bikers talked to the kid on the ATV. And then an anti-social biker in sports gear raced by the kids' parents. Surprised, the mom backed up, tripped and fell down; the dad yelled after the biker and helped his wife up. The kids continued to race around.

A park ranger approached and spoke with the parents. I heard the man say something like, "There is no one around here. They are not endangering anyone." The ranger exercised his discretion, for which he has some sovereign immunity handed down by kings of yore, and the event continued.

Two obedient kids came up the hill with skateboards in hand instead of underfoot. They expressed bitter disappointment that they could not roll down the side of the hill under repair, but then they had a great time rolling down the other side.

I was really enjoying the whole scene. I think people will agree that city officials just want people to enjoy the parks. They put up some signs with rules. They are not too keen on enforcing them. Yes, if they confiscated the bikes and gave them to charity, if they publicly caned violators for violations, the rules would be obeyed except by innocent tourists who had not seen the beatings on television or had not been warned by their travel agents.

I decided then and there to send Mr. Rebar a constructive criticism letter with this positive suggestion: Find an even better way to allow people to do what they want to do. Put some sort of artificial turf on the sides of the hill for people to have fun on. Convert the area at the bottom of the hill into a little course for kids; maybe rent them plastic cars at the concession shop. Build out a cross training area on the lawn and book professional trainers to conduct classes. Station two safety ambassadors to attend to the little free amusement park.

I know, I would not enjoy seeing so many violations. Maybe I would take an exercise class to improve mind-body coordination.

Miami Beach Has Gone To The Dogs

"For those who are offended at the lightness and pedantry of this subject, I would have them consider that I do not set myself for the first example of this kind, but that the same has been oft done by many considerable authors. For thus several ages since, Homer wrote of no more weighty a subject than of a war between the frogs and mice, Virgil of a gnat and a pudding cake, and Ovid of a nut. Polycrates commended the cruelty of Busiris; and Isocrates, who corrects him forth is, did as much for the injustice of Glaucus. Favorinus extolled Thersites, and wrote in praise of a quartaneague. Synesius pleaded in behalf of baldness; and Lucian defended a sipping fly. Seneca drollingly related the deifying of Claudius; Plutarch the dialogue betwixt Gryllus and Ulysses; Lucian and Apuleius the story of an ass; and somebody else records the last will of a hog, of which St Hierom makes mention. So that if they please, let themselves think the worst of me, and fancy to themselves that I was all this while a playing at push-pin, or riding astride on a hobby-horse. For how unjust is it, if when we allow different recreations to each particular course of life, we afford no diversion to studies; especially when trifles may be a whet to more serious thoughts, and comical matters may be so treated of, as that a reader of ordinary sense may possibly thence reap more advantage than from some more big and stately argument: as while one in a long-winded oration descants in commendation of rhetoric or philosophy, another in a fulsome harangue sets forth the praise of his nation, a third makes a zealous invitation to a holy war with the Turks, another confidently sets up for a fortune-teller, and a fifth states questions upon mere impertinences. But as nothing is more childish than to handle a serious subject in a loose, wanton style, so is there nothing more pleasant than so to treat of trifles, as to make them seem nothing less than what their name imports. Erasmus." *In Praise of Folly*

2015 South Beach

His dog Earl is Mayor Philip Levine's best friend. We do not begrudge him that. A dog is often a man's only friend because it is loves him faithfully no matter what, even if abused. Furthermore, a dogged candidate will get a lot of votes.

The mayor claims that it was not his personal wealth and friendship with the Clintons that won 50.8% of the vote and the 17 votes that avoided a runoff against Michael Gongora at the last election. His money may have purchased a majority on the commission, making him a strong mayor of a city with a weak mayor charter, but his money was meaningless to the dogs who won the day for him.

The illustrious media mogul and real estate developer said he knocked on 6,000 doors, heard dogs barking at 75 percent of the residences, and promoted a bark beach for neglected North Beach, which he conceived to be a sort of sister city to popular South Beach. After he got elected, he got that done fast because you do not say no to the mayor and get away with it given his penchant for fascistic governance. The project was evidently celebrated on the North Beach sand outside of the confines of a fenced-in dog park, raising some concerns about the contamination of the beach with dog waste. The new bark beach park is enclosed and attended to by the city for a modest annual fee to its users.

A local ordinance prohibits animals other than human beings from being present on beaches other than specially protected areas, the North Beach bark park being the only bark beach park thus far.

Why the prohibition? According to the Environmental Protection Agency, a single gram of dog waste can contain 23 million fecal coliform bacteria, which are known to cause cramps, diarrhea, intestinal illness, and serious kidney disorders in humans. Dog feces are one of the most common carriers of the following diseases: Whipworms; Hookworms; Roundworms; Tapeworms; Parvo; Corona; Giardiasis; Salmonellosis; Cryptosporidiosis; Campylobacteriosis. The EPA estimates that two or three days' worth of droppings from a population of about 100 dogs would contribute enough bacteria to temporarily close a bay, and all watershed areas within 20 miles of it, to swimming and shell fishing.

Nonetheless, the Levine advertisement for his reelection, featuring him with his dog at the South Pointe beach's iconic lighthouse lifeguard station, is promoting the unrestricted presence of dogs on the beach contrary to existing ordinance and federal health advisories.

The advertisements have been running for several weeks on television networks. The TV spots have been referred to the city's code enforcement officials with a suggestion that the mayor be fined for each broadcast featuring his violation of the ordinance. A gentleman of his substance would willingly pay the fines, or have a political action committee pay them, instead of ordering his henchman the city manager to declare the area violated an ex post facto bark beach, by virtue of the dictatorial power written into the ordinance by the mayor's majority on the commission.

It is unknown at this time whether the funding for the television commercial is related to the so-called Dirty PAC Money Affair. The mayor is rich and able to fund his own campaign as he did before; a couple of million dollars for a job that pays less than $10,000 per year is chump change for him. The glory of basking in vanity magazines and slick media advertisements and going on perhaps to become an ambassador to Saudi Arabia for Hilary is well worth it.

A civic-minded South Beach resident who frequents the beach informed me that she has been threatened for politely reminding people with dogs on the beach that all animals except humans are prohibited on the beach. She said that one woman cursed at her, pulled out her cell phone and called two men out of a beach residence, and they approached her in an aggressive manner. Sometimes, she said, the same people have a dozen or so dogs on the beach in the mornings, running in the sand and swimming in the water.

Furthermore, despite efforts to tame South Pointe Park with police patrols, and the installation of a security guard at the new pier, she said dogs are running around loose on the beach itself as policemen sit on their ATVs elsewhere in the park to chat since not much is happening besides dogs on the beach and running around off leash in the park.

My informant, whose name I withhold to protect her from retaliation, which is the primitive rule rather than the exception in the city, said that she loves dogs, and longs to have one herself since her ex-husband, enraged by her love for her dog, bashed its brains out against the wall in front of her.

Her own breeding, she said, has caused her to be far more concerned with cleanliness and hygiene than most people, and to politely advise others to abide by public hygiene standards. And for that we cannot blame her. Indeed, sanitation is fundamental to religion as is evident in primitive cleansing rituals.

"They have dog parks off the beach and should use them. I do not want myself and others to be infected by dog waste. They should obey the law."

Miami Beach residents are not known for their social conscience unless that conscience includes the entire animal kingdom set upside down in ethical terms. Ethologists have persuaded themselves that human conscience is rooted in base forms of social life despite the prejudice of libertarians and anarchists that individuals possess an innate freedom of conscience, an inner light or an intuitive, private access to enlightenment from the highest authority.

The Knight Ridder Foundation has reported that most new residents are attracted to Miami as a place to live privately without social pressures. Thus a few Miami Beach people who do associate in groups have obtained political power over an apathetic population of 100,000. Those groups are dominated by the affluent residents residing in the multimillion dollar condominiums on the fringes of the beach, especially in South Beach. A few thousand votes will win local elections. The unincorporated South of Fifth Neighborhood Association, whose economic elite has supported the continuing conversion of the neighborhood by developers into a condominium retreat for ultra-high-income individuals, is the mayor's ardent supporter. In any event, the mayor's self-involved attitude, that anything he does or supports is absolutely great, and that all dissent must be stifled, strikes a chord with many South of Fifth Street residents.

My informant said she made the "mistake" of stopping to advise a woman on the South Pointe beach that dogs are not permitted on the beach.

"I was very courteous, spoke softly and smiled, but the beautiful modele screamed at me, called me a terrorist, and threatened to knock me down, so I went over to the officers chatting on their ATVs nearby. One of them said they were supposed to be 'lenient' in the mornings, so they did not enforce the law. I said leniency was against the hygiene law, and that this woman had threatened to knock me down twice just for mentioning it. The other officer agreed, so they went over to her. She saw them coming, and removed some of her clothing as they approached—a female strategy—but when they started talking to her, she screamed at them. I tried to take a close-up picture, but one of the officers ordered me not to take pictures. I thought he would arrest me if I did, so I was frightened and left."

I went over to the beach the next morning to follow up on her story. It was already 90 degrees and as humid as the Amazon.

First of all, I discovered that South Beach lifeguards became so exasperated by the rudeness of dog owners on the beach that they have given up on saying anything to them at all.

People do not even bother to get phony service dog tags now that the mayor has legitimized dogs on the beach. The law does not require any proof anyway; all one can do is ask what kind of service the dog is providing. I recalled how frustrated the manager at the Publix was with people who allow their so-called service dogs to urinate and defecate in the shopping carts and hand baskets.

So the lifeguards now focus on people in the water since their core mission is to save them from drowning. The code of silence prevents them from speaking about the conduct of police officers.

A security officer, speaking under condition of anonymity as several dogs ran past us onto the sand—including the famous dog whose wealthy owner paid so many tickets that orders were allegedly given to ignore further violations—related that dog owners who live in the neighborhood had yelled and screamed at him as well, and had even spit on him. He said he did not care if the famous dog's owner got $2,000 in tickets; he should get $6,000 or more in tickets until he starts obeying the law.

We spoke of how Commissioner Michael Grieco, a criminal defense attorney who frequents the park, had been helpful with quality of life issues.

"He has done some good," I admitted. "Mayor Levine, however, is advertising dogs on the sand at South Pointe, so Michael goes along with it because, in a way, he is the mayor's chief dog. He should growl once in a while, and even bark, show some independence if he wants to be mayor. And he is deliberately blind to the city manager's incompetence, perhaps because the city manager recommends whatever the mayor wants because his job depends on the mayor's majority. A provision was made in the ordinance to allow the city manager to dictate the create dog parks anywhere he wants."

I did not mind referring to the commissioner as a dog, since I was told that I had been called a dog by a prominent neighborhood association member as a result of my efforts to get the construction and real estate sign blight in the neighborhood eliminated. Several wealthy residents, virtual stooges for the developers, had scoffed at my belief that signage should be permitted and architects and contractors licensed in Florida.

As a matter of fact, I am a dog lover myself in the right setting. For me, that is the countryside. My favorite stories in my childhood were personifications of wild dogs running the countryside, occasionally joined by domesticated farm dogs. My father thought it pathetic that people had come to love their dogs more than people, and said they should be canned and sent to Asia to feed the poor. Dogs eat humans, and humans eat dogs, he noted.

SIGN South Pointe Park (OFF-LEASH) 1 Washington Avenue Sunrise - 10:00 a.m. • Daily 6:00 p.m. - 9:00 p.m. • Monday - Friday only DOGS PERMITTED OFF-LEASH IN THIS AREA ONLY It is a violation to permit dogs to run at large in any other area of this park, or in this designated area at any time other than posted, or to fail to clean up after your dog*. Violations are subject to fines and strictly enforced. Hours of operations only in specified area (fence-less grass area south and west of the Washington Avenue entry plaza).

I strolled towards the off-leash area in the park, a short distance from the beach. I noticed several dogs along the way, off leash in the rest of the park as usual. The off-leash laws are not and have never been strictly enforced. In fact, Miami Beach has a long history of selective enforcement of various municipal ordinances. Violators in South Pointe Park get occasional warnings, and are rarely ticketed. After all, these residents are the power elite that elected officials prefer not to offend. People do not bring dogs over from Miami to run in the park and on the beach.

I espied two men and a woman with their dogs in the designated off-leash area. I asked them why there was no dog run as advertised by the city for bark parks.

There has never had been a dog run here, one gentleman said, but at least it is the only bark park in the city without a fence around it.

I said I remembered a great controversy over putting a hedge around it, at which he said he and the other two were having a very important conversation, so get lost. They must be conspiring to make more money, I conjectured as I went on my way, because that is almost all I hear people talking about in the neighborhood. Donald Trump, Martha Steward, Leona Helmsley, Philip Levine, among others, claim they would do on wrong or are independent because they have plenty of money; there is, however, never enough money.

Transcripts from the Great Hedge Controversy of 2012 include the park director's testimony that the off-leash area was working well for 18 months because residents were providing their own monitoring. The only resident who dared to expose the nonsense about the protective hedge was one Jean Kulick.

Before reporting her testimony, the city was careful to disqualify her: "Ms. Kulick did not offer any credentials into the record to indicate any background or training with regard to park design, maintenance, or management."

"Her generalized testimony included that the multiple use of the Park has been seriously unbalanced by the extension of the off-leash hours. Ms. Kulick also opined that due to the climate with no rain, the vestige of feces left by dogs in the Park is dangerous. She also disagreed with other record testimony that dog owners are self-policing and referred to them as "distasteful" and "shabbily rude" to the security guards and that hedges would not be able to cope with the dog situation. Ms. Kulick also speculated that the Park will deteriorate, while also commenting that the Parks Department does a "brilliant job" and "they've maintained it beautifully." Additionally, without any photographic or other evidence, Ms. Kulick opined that the regular use of the Park grass by off-leash dogs would leave urine stains and that it would be a dust bowl."

Since then, city contractor Superior Landscaping has been replacing the brand new grass installed in the park although people did have difficulty seeing anything wrong with it. The multimillion dollar project, called the Grassdoggle, is said to be necessary because Superior did not have enough money in its coffers.

No credentials in park management were needed from another resident:

"Larry Wyman, another resident in the neighborhood and on the board of the SoFiK9 organization, also testified. He noted the success of the South Pointe Park off-leash area and that the issues described by Ms. Kulick where pretty much the exception and not the rule. Mr. Wyman testified to the tremendous community that has developed amongst dog owners who visit the Park and that the off leash program has worked better than as described in the comments by Ms. Kulick. In addition, Mr. Wyman noted that the Park has sprinklers and the alleged problem regarding dog urine was not really an issue. Based on his observations, the use that the grass is taking in the off-leash area is no different than the use the grass is taking in other areas of the Park where picnicking, playing soccer, and other activities occur."

Anyone who bothers to look can see dogs off leash in the park, and they can take plenty of pictures of violations as well.

Carl Schmitt, the doctor of jurisprudence who justified the suspension of the Weimar constitution for the National Socialist Party and whose protégé Leo Strauss was admired by President Bush's strategists, said that to get anything done in a democracy, given its conflicting interests, one must lie. Wherefore the world is covered with bullshit.

Suffice it to say that everyone who frequents South Pointe Park and who are concerned with hygiene knows well enough not to roll around in the grass. Hilda Fernandez, an assistant city manager during the Great Hedge Controversy, pointed out that dogs will do their thing whether on or off leash, and so will their owners.

Now that the mayor has taken the law into his own hands to condone the presence of animals besides humans on the beach, it is advisable to wear shoes, to avoid contact with the sand, and not to swim in the water. Travel agencies should be notified, and advisory signs should be posted for the protection of the public.

Continuing on my way, I noticed a woman smiling lovingly at her off-leash dog, and he seemed to be smiling back. The sight was charming, really.

A fuzzy little brown dog ran up to get a whiff of me. So cute!

A man came out of the Mondrian with a dog, turned it loose to run around and do its thing, and then went back to his condo without cleaning up. I paused there for a while to read some of Thomas Mann's 'A Man and His Dog.'

"Here for a while I stroll along the paths, and Bashan revels in the freedom of unlimited level space, galloping across and across the lawns like mad with his body inclined in a centrifugal plane; sometimes, barking with mingled pleasure and exasperation, he pursues a bird which flutters as though spellbound, but perhaps on purpose to tease him, along the ground just in front of his nose. But if I sit on the bench he is at my side at once and takes up a position on one of my feet. For it is a law of his being that he only runs about when I am in motion too; that when I settle down he follows suit. There seems no obvious reason for this practice; but Bashan never fails to conform to it. I get an odd, intimate, and amusing sensation from having him sit on my foot and warm it with the blood-heat of his body. A pervasive feeling of sympathy and good cheer fills me, as almost invariably when in his company and looking at things from his angle."

Man is a self-conscious animal who makes a god of himself and sets himself against the animal that he is. What we have here, I concluded, is a conflict in need of reconciliation, a conflict between god and god spelled backwards.

Southe Pointe Gloome

"Breathe deep the gathering gloom, watch lights fade from every room." (Graeme Edge). Sunday was a gloomy yet beautiful day. It had dawned on me in the morn, while reflecting on the past in bed, that history is indeed a serious mistake, including watching Inherit the Wind before falling asleep. Every memory I dredged up was painful. I found nothing bittersweet, nothing recalled from long ago to long for, and everything to regret, except unconditional love for a friend, who was absent. In her presence there was some hope in my remorse for the rapidly dwindling future, wherein I might somehow slightly compensate for my faults, including the original sin of being born individual, before venturing alone to that Better Place funereal preachers speak of; as if no place, or, in a word, utopia, were better than this place; wherefore Nothing, the absence of anything at all, is perfect.

Thus it was in a darkling mood that I greeted the gloom and proceeded to mark the overcastted day with my usual Sunday walk around South Pointe Park. No matter how dismal the day may be, it may be brightened by the art of living. Pliny, according to Bayle's Dictionary, said, "It was an invariable rule with Apelles never to pass a day without exercising his art, at least by one stroke of his pencil; which passed from him in a proverb." Horace quoted the proverb as: "Nulla dies abeat, quin lines ducta supersit." That is: Let no day pass without drawing at least one line to show for it. The succinct version employed by writers is, 'Nulla dies sine linea.'

Having found fault with myself at length, I naturally found fault with others when entering the park. A Bike and Roll guide was leading a Segway tour into the park despite a new ordinance prohibiting the "diabolical devices," as one resident called them, from being operated there and on other walkways near the beachfront. One of the Segway riders started rolling backwards; the guide ran and stopped the Segway before it rolled over the ledge, reminding me of how the investor who purchased the Segway business had been killed when he went off a cliff on the product.

Ironically, the rather charming young guide told the German tourists that it was illegal for them to ride Segways in the park. They scoffed at the very notion that such a thing would be illegal in America. She said the police might catch them. I laughed out loud at that because the lifestyle ordinances are rarely if ever proactively enforced. Heck, there was not a uniformed cop or code officer or private security guard around that morning. Unsupervised code officers and security guards tend to goof off when they are at the park while the rules posted on signs around them are disobeyed.

Despite this scofflawry and my fault-finding tendency, I was inclined to tolerate if not forgive the breach because of a few lines spoken about my critical avocation, muckraking, in Inherit the Wind. The Bike and Roll guide and her group did block the walkway at times, but she had simply taken them to a spot near the entrance to remark on the beautiful sights and to take photographs. I had worked in the travel business myself at her age, and she was handling her group very well despite the infraction. I would send the images I took to a commissioner, who had sponsored the Segway ban, to see what he thought about the matter. Since he is a criminal defense attorney, maybe he will find some of the evidence exculpatory.

I continued onward. It looked like it was going to rain cats and dogs. Maybe that is why I saw only one dog, a little brown one, instead of the usual dozen or so. And on the Sunday prior, which was actually sunny, I noticed that the Lighthouse Dog Park had been dug up, so that might have something to do with the dearth of dogs around the time I take my walks.

Amazingly, the little brown dog was on a leash! I was so astonished that I had to congratulate the man. He turned out to be Mike from Colorado, the 71-year old father of a man who lives in the older Continuum condominium. I explained how I had observed a code compliance officer sitting in his car for some time as several dogs were running around unleashed, and, when I got a copy of his report for that period, I discovered that he was on so-called dog patrol, reporting that he saw no dog violations, observed 17 dogs on leashes, and had, curiously, indoctrinated several of their owners to the dog leash law.

"Dogs should be on leashes," Mike said. "You never know what they might do."

I agreed, noting how I had taken a picture of a man chasing a runaway dog after the code officer parked his car with its rear facing the park. The officer could have seen it in his rear view mirror, but he was too busy fiddling with his phone or computer.

Mike said that his son had a Doberman as well as the dog he was walking, but he did not want to bring both dogs out at once as his son was wont to do.

I just had to tell my Doberman story, about Liz, a Manhattan call girl who would eventually save enough money to become a vet and establish her own clinic down South. She liked to carry a boa in her purse, keeping it well fed with mice in her West Side studio. She had two Dobermans. They slept in her clothes closet or were confined there when bad. Sunday strollers parted like the Red Sea had done for Moses when Liz walked to Central Park on West 72nd Street with a ferocious-looking dog on each side. She took them off leash to swim in the lake as usual one day, and sat down under a tree. A vagrant grabbed her, pushed her down and proceeded to rip her panties off. She gave the attack signal to the dogs, a loud, peculiar sneezing sound. He lost an eye, an ear, and half his nose. There were no witnesses. Despite the bruises and ripped panties resulting from the assault, battery, and attempted rape, it was "he said, she said." The assailant was released. A felony charge had been brought against Liz, later reduced to violation of the leash law.

"You know what animal I fear the most?" Mike asked, after hearing my true tale.

"What?"

"You, I fear you the most. You might shake my hand with one hand and pick my pocket or stab me with the other. A lion will walk by a lamb without harming it if it is not hungry...."\

"I know what you mean. I remember there was a covered cage at the Honolulu Zoo that had a sign saying, 'The World's Most Dangerous Animal.' When you looked into the window, you saw yourself in a mirror."

"That's right. I am afraid of you," Mike confirmed.

"I would not hurt you, but I take that a little personally because I am a journalist, a cynical and skeptical one at that, and I saw Inherit the Wind last evening. Have you seen it?"

"I don't recall."

"It is a propaganda film that used to be shown to high school kids, based on the Scopes Monkey Trial. A great deal of it is misleading. In fact it exaggerates the virtues of science over religion in its fictitious personifications of William Jennings Bryan and Clarence Darrow, and entirely misses the crucial point which neither theology nor biology is needed to prove. In any event, I was struck as if by lightning by the quotation inserted from Proverbs, that....excuse me, I am having difficulty remembering it now, which is something I must do in order to be a righteous person. Alas, my memory had been failing me of late. I even forgot the name of a man I wrote a book about. Thankfully, I can still remember five of the Ten Commandments, the last five of the popular order, so maybe I'm an atheist."

Mike smiled as I paused and struggled to recall the awful truth sunk into me the night before.

"Oh, yes, I remember: 'He that troubleth is own house shall inherit the wind.'

"And I was further troubled by the scene after the trial, where Darrow is portrayed as turning to Mencken, the cynical reporter who happens to be a literary hero of mine, beautifully acted by the great dancer, Gene Kelly, to ask him: 'Where will your loneliness lead you? No one will come to your funeral.' Mencken replied that Darrow would be there to defend his right to be alone.

"I felt very alone at that moment," I confessed to the stranger and his dog, "not only all alone, which can be a good thing, but lonely, washed up on the beach after two failed marriages, a cynical old man preoccupied with criticizing everything under the sun at the very end of his days, particularly the government of this city. It may be impossible for me to recover, to cover myself with a rationale, say, that I seek to expose the truth, when in doing so I place myself above my own awful truth, the very reality I would avoid by distancing myself from it to write about it."

"Man is an unpredictable animal," declared Mike, nodding sagely, as if I were a fool judged by the heart of a wise man. "If you see my son walking along here with this dog and his Doberman, say hello for me."

I continued on with my walk, thinking that I, who had lately been following in the footsteps of the muckrakers of old, would be absolutely alone at my funeral, without a soul to mourn my passing. I would later read from Clarence Darrow's autobiography that Bryan had a hero's funeral, which of course he could not personally enjoy.

"Mr. Bryan lost his hold in Tennessee when he testified in court," wrote Darrow, "but his tragic end, which came so soon after, restored him to their hearts. Great throngs of people visited the little house in Dayton to take a last look at their hero. All the people of that section seemed to be at the funeral. Then he was taken by a special car to Arlington. The train stopped at all the towns on the route. It took a long time to make the journey, for everywhere a large concourse of mourning friends stood waiting, sometimes for hours, with wreaths and furled flags, in sorrowful remembrance of their lost leader."

I suppose we should all worry about how many people will come to our funerals. A nurse of fundamentalist persuasion once told me that people who died friendless, all alone in hospitals, deserved their fate, and would probably roast eternally in hellfire unless someone came to their funeral. I must find out how many people attended the funerals of Darrow and Mencken in order to determine their stature in comparison to that of Bryan. Scopes himself was not as great as depicted in Inherit the Wind. He was a coach substituting for a teacher, and did not teach evolutionism during that two weeks, but he agreed to be arrested and charged with the crime in order to test the statute. I must find out how many people came to his funeral.

One of the most interesting funerals I have read about so far is that of assassinated President James Garfield. What he could have done as president augmented the mourning already considerable due to his fame as a Civil War general and civil rights congressman. Perhaps I shall be mourned for what I could have been, a significant representative of the human tragedy, crucified by reality and ideality crossed, the crisis underlying human nature, the hypocrisy, et cetera et cetera. And then, if only one person attends my funeral, my soul shall be saved from hellfire while my body is being incinerated.

Oh, the Gloom! Yet here is a bright spot at the end of the walkway. Reconstruction of the pier on the beach end of South Pointe Park is almost finished. I wondered if the Cubans would come back to fish after all these years. Or is it illegal to fish? And there is another bright spot, the lifeguard station, fashioned like a lighthouse, standing at the foot of the Continuum towers.

I was disappointed to learn during a visit to the Planning Department that the lifeguard stations were going to be replaced by stations designed by the architect who had designed the previous ones.

Politics: It is de rigueur since the election to hate the previous city manager with a passion, hence to undo what he has done whether it deserves undoing or not. That includes the plans for the grandest convention center known to mankind, now scrapped with a vengeance.

Beach Rescue lifeguards certainly had many reasons to despise "Boss" Gonzalez. Pay was cut. Lifeguard stations were run down, used as toilets. Lifeguards had to build a station out of scrap wood after it was destroyed by a storm. I was present as an emergency crew tried to save a tourist drowned New Year's Eve 2005 in one of the so-called blind spots, where there are no stations, in broad daylight, and saw his little kids taken away utterly bewildered. Of course the event was not covered by the mainstream press.

"The city manager does not listen to us," one rescuer at the drowning scene complained about the blind spot. "The only chance of getting anything done in Miami Beach is to get ahold of the new elected commission, Matti Bower," said another. After I reported on the drowning, the lifeguards said they were ordered not to talk to me, then told me everything,

The stations were eventually remodeled or replaced, and the lighthouse station has become a world-renowned South Beach icon. Not a single city official responded to my entreaties to save it. I asked the famous neighborhood activist for assistant; he did not respond, perhaps because the new regime adopted him as a political operative, and it is de rigueur for the new regime to hate anything the old regime did.

The lighthouse lifeguard had raised red flags in the gloom, signaling danger. I took some pictures. The bottom flag, indicating that the water was closed to the public, was upside down. The lifeguard appeared and fixed it, explaining that the warning was up because of the gloom, making it difficult to spot swimmers in distress. Several people were swimming in the perfectly calm water. As the wind whipped up and darker clouds moved near, he blew his whistle repeatedly, waving for them to get out of the water.

He had scant time to talk. He did say that Jimmy Morales had visited lifeguards, that he is a very nice man. Mayor Philip Levine also visited, and said that a million or so would be budgeted for improvements, and then he walked eighty blocks, visiting every station along the way. I was incredulous about the eighty blocks, so I marked my calendar to attempt to confirm that information—the mayor's office normally responds positively only to mainstream media, previously identified by the major's campaign as "legitimate."

People were grabbing beach chairs and running for cover as the gusts mounted. I noted the direction of the wind and the appearance of the clouds, judging that it would not pour as expected—I was correct, for what it's worth.

I spotted lifeguard Lt. Leigh Emerson-Smith, a thirty-year Beach Rescue veteran, passing by in her Rescue vehicle. I flagged her down.

"How incredibly beautiful this gloomy day is!" I yelled against the wind I seemed destined to inherit. "So how is the new administrating treating Beach Rescue?"

"Fire Department chiefs have been replaced. Beach Rescue is now treated with a great deal of respect. Jimmy Morales is a great guy. Pay cuts are restored. Promotions are in abeyance. We have money for uniforms. One-point-two million is budgeted for improvements. Four stations will be added to the twenty-nine stations we have."

Well, maybe there is light at the end of this political tunnel, after all, I silently mused, provided that the city manager is not too nice to the wrong people. He is a novice at civic management, yet he seems to be a fast learner. The new mayor is not so nice, so no problem there. Police officers have told me they do not like the way he looks down on them, as if they were employees of his private company. Maybe he will learn to be half as nice as Jimmy, and, most importantly, to rid himself of his childish vindictiveness towards anyone who disagrees with him.

"Don't work too hard!" I exclaimed as Leigh drove away.

"That is what we are here for!" she called back.

"Yeah, but look out, that can get you transferred or terminated around here!"

Aw shucks. I am too cynical. I had better watch out myself if I want someone to come to my funeral, if there is one, to save my soul from eternal hellfire.

Miami Beach Laws Made To Be Broken

Osleydi Cobas of Alliance Security certainly had her hands full at South Pointe Park in 2014as she pedaled up and down the boardwalk along Government Cut last Sunday. The park was chock full of scofflaws and persons ignorant of the laws.

The first thing I noticed upon entry into the park was the illegal sign reported to the Code Compliance Department several weeks before it became illegible due to neglect: "Another Quality Job By Superior Landscaping & Lawn Service Inc. 1-800-759-4156.

Here is yet another contractor, I reflected, that is either ignorant of the laws that govern its trade for the safety and welfare of the public, or is so ashamed of its state contractor's license that it fails to put it on its advertisements as required by law.

Never mind, they are protected by the police power, i.e. the city government. Code compliance officers simply thumb their noses at this kind of violation in plain sight, unless someone risks retaliation by complaining.

I wondered what other laws Superior might regularly break behind the signs. One of my confidential sources at city hall expressed the same concern along with doubts about the safety of the procedures followed by this plumber and landscaper, assigned to remediate the faults of a previous contractor and, additionally, to perpetuate the Grass Boondoggle, replacing the lovely grass with new grass.

Why, I noticed that Superior had hung another advertisement of its ignorance or disobedience on the temporary fences, this one facing the channel, obviously for the benefit of the affluent class that sails by on yachts and cruise ships.

I had already pointed out to government officials the probably unpermitted signs of New Construction Inc. and ASR Construction, both absent license numbers, placed on and in front of the construction project on Fisher Island directly across Government Cut from Superior's handiwork.

Fisher Island reportedly has the highest per capital income in this great nation of ours. I asked high city officials in July of this year if the City of Miami Beach had jurisdiction over Fisher Island construction or whether Fisher Island was a government unto itself. I noted that David Weston, a fire inspector fired for complaining about irregularities, had insisted there were irregularities when he inspected construction on Fisher Island, was then was banned from the island with a finger in the chest. I said I thought he was treated rudely. He then participated in my report on the Fisher Island signage to say that what occurred was not merely "rudeness" but "criminal," in his opinion, so he reported it to law enforcement and to Joe Centorino, the current director of the county ethics commission.

High city officials did not respond to my inquiry. However, New Construction proudly printed its license number on the sign since then, perhaps at the behest of the State regulators whom I had copied. ASR is remiss. Six signs were arrayed on the project this Sunday: two ASR signs in front and one on the building itself; one NET Construction sign and one Kobi Karp sign in front, both with license numbers; one sign indistinguishable from my distant position without magnification.

Let not the reader imagine that this disarray at my entrance into South Pointe Park was ruining the incredibly beautiful, sunny day for me—I do not attend church on Sun Day because I prefer to worship the Sun. No, I am sure that my day was even sunnier than it was for people in the dark about local regulations or those who could care less about them. I have no axe to grind with the violators themselves because their violations are condoned by the most egregious of scofflaws, i.e. negligent public officials. I have seen Superior workers keeping the city landscape clean; they do a good job. I have myself been a loyal right-hand man of developers and contractors. No, pointing out irregularities is my way of shining the light on the government's legendary bureaucratic ass, which grows quite large in a subtropical clime rich in rice and beans, bananas and mangoes.

I continued happily on my way on this resplendent Sunday. A photographer had strewn himself, his partner, and his equipment across that way, obstructing both pedestrians and bicyclists, one of whom was shouting, "You're taking up all the space!"

The photographer and his partner were obtuse. Why should they care? This is a free city, is it not? Maybe not the 3.00 World, but it is perhaps 2.25 World.

I approached the photographer in a friendly manner, and asked, humorously, as I pointed out the whole array blocking the sidewalk, "By the way, do you have a permit to block the sidewalk with all this?"

"Do you have a permit for that coffee you are drinking or the black shirt you wear?" was his flippant reply, so I left him behind.

I button-holed Osleydi Cobas along the way, and asked her if she would mind asking the photographer not to take up the whole sidewalk. I said the equipment gave me the impression he was a professional, yet his conduct gave me cause to doubt that he had a permit.

"Sure," she said. "I'll check it out. They usually have permits."

As I approached the recently reopened pier, informally dubbed the Jorge Gonzalez South Pointe Pier to honor the former city manager, I noticed tourists on Segways led by a Bike & Roll tour guide. They stopped for a photo shoot at the pier, where the tour guide posed for my photo.

Ms. Cobas had returned to say that the photographer was indeed blocking the sidewalk, and she concurred with my characterization of him as "flippant," so she reported her observation to Code Compliance. It was not long before she received a call from the Compliance officer, who said the photographer had a license.

But that was not the main issue, said Ms. Cobas. "The issue, as I said, was blocking the sidewalk."

I made a note to obtain the record to see if a name and permit number was obtained, and if a warning was given not to obstruct traffic. Code Compliance officers have had a marked preference for reporting "No Violation" in our liberal domain.

Ms. Cobas was amused by my conversation with Ben, the Bike & Roll tour guide, during my own photo shoot, with my cheap cell phone, especially when I said: "Incidentally, Segways and other motorized vehicles have been illegal here and along the beach boardwalk since the first of July, I think."

"Oh, I'm sorry, I did not know. I have only been here two weeks. A security guard told me yesterday that Segways are okay here."

Not so, indicated Ms. Cobas with a negative shake of her head.

"I called the office," he responded, "and the manager said she would look into it."

"You mean the young, pretty lady who leads some of the tours?"

"Yeah."

"Maybe she is the escort whom I informed Commissioner Michael Grieco, a supporter of the ban, that she was flouting the new law some time ago in the park. Actually, I was in the tour business for several years, myself, so I have sympathy for your business, which set up for these tours only to have Segways banned. However, the welfare and safety of the public is of concern, and Segways are dangerous. I watched a lady on a Bike & Roll tour in this park roll backwards a few weeks ago, and she nearly went off the ledge. Do you know how the purchaser of Segway met his death?"

"Yes,"

"These machines are heavy. Someone I know was injured when he was hit in the back by one."

"We had a Segway incident here last week," Ms. Cobas volunteered.

"I did not know," said the guide, anxiously.

"Security observes and reports. By the time Code Compliance is called, you will be gone, so a 'No Violation' record will be created. The commissioners create and recreate these laws and proudly take credit for them, but they are made to be broken, and are broken time and time again because the unelected city manager is responsible for enforcement, not them, so your company does not have much to worry about."

Indeed, since the new ordinance was passed the Segway and Trikes tours have actually increased, making a joke of the power of the City Commission, which, according to Commissioner Grieco, follows the recommendations of City Manager Jimmy Morales "almost blindly."

As the Segway tour departed, Ms. Cobas was kept busy stopping people from entering the pier on bikes or with their dogs. She said sometimes the Park Department stationed someone there. Even so, that person would go off on other business often. The city officials do not want big signs ruining the view, she said.

One big sign filled with finely printed Do Nots was mounted by the pier. I had to put on my glasses to read the sign and find the clauses prohibiting bikes and dogs. As I did so, the officer had to stop a dozen bicyclists. A megaphone should be part of her equipment.

Ms. Cobas complained about the size of the "Pedestrians Only" sign at the bottom of the side-walked hill nearby.

Guide laughing at sign before he led tour up the hill on Segways

I said that tour guides know about the signs, even giving them the finger in photo shoots. Others follow unruly leaders. People who care only about themselves and what they want to do and who are aware of them scoff at them, flaunting their disobedience as if that were the American Way.

Why not? Government is evil, is it not? Laws are made to be broken. If someone complains, hand out a warning so the violators can just do it again, and say something like, "Our objective is compliance not punishment." I resisted a temptation to say how this so-called Western attitude was helping organizations recruit terrorists in the Middle East.

The Alliance Security officer had not left the pier for 5 minutes before a man on a motor scooter whizzed by at about twenty miles-per-hour. I caught a glimpse of a Trikes tour entering the park, so I went after them in hopes of getting pictures and an interview. They were travelling too fast for me to catch up. I did encounter a detective on his all-terrain vehicle under a tree near the garage in the park. He was busy chatting on the phone so I very briefly asked if the career thief had been caught yet (no) and kept on going.

I resolved to check the Code again the next week. Maybe the new prohibition on motorized vehicles in certain areas along the beach has been rescinded. Several people have told me that the tours are ongoing with a vengeance. I warned the commissioners that it would not be enforced. Why make laws meant to be broken, anyway? People just turn their backs on them.

Permit Fixing Permit Doctor

Jimmy 'Nice Guy' Morales

Manager

City of Miami Beach

24 November 2017

Re Permit Fixing and Permit Doctor

Mr. Morales:

We had much to give thanks for this Thanksgiving, did we not? We have a change of leadership in Zimbabwe, and Dan Gelber, the brand new mayor of Miami Beach who said he would not have run for the post without you already ensconced as city manager, is regarded as a "messiah." So I take this opportunity to raise a lingering issue.

The firm doing business as "Permit Doctor," as you know, leases space adjacent to city hall for its business, is very cozy with the city officials who issue permits. The company, apparently exempted from the signage ordinances governing other businesses, has completely ignored the old signage permit ordinance requiring each sign, other than construction signs part of a fencing wrap, to bear a permit number by way of decal and expiration date. Any sign not a part of the construction shell (fencing wrap) approved by the Planning Department had to bear a permit decal or was not permitted.

Enforcement of the permitting requirements for the shell advertising as well as signs requiring decals, to wit those affixed to the shells and free standing signs, was virtually ignored by your Code Compliance Department as a waste of resources, wherefore violations were ignored unless someone vigorously pressed a complaint, and even then inquiries about Permit Doctor signs were not responded to.

Permit Doctor advertising signs now appear throughout the city on windows and on fences. As usual, none of them bear permit decals, which they should have had under the old ordinance since they are not part of construction shells approved by the Planning Department.

Now I have noticed that the revised signage ordinances in the Municode does not even have an Administrative Section, and does not mention marking signs with a permit number as evidence of permitting, without which they are not permitted. The new codification does have some improvements, but it is sloppily drafted in several respects. My discussions of the subject were evidently not even considered because of the public exclusion policy.

This apparent lack in the code is disturbing because if true it dovetails with what appears to be a change of philosophy since Mayor Levine used his fortune to subvert the City Charter to prostitute power seekers and render himself a strong mayor and preclude participation by the general public, especially that faction he designated as "screamers and yellers" who would have to "wait until the next election to be heard."

And that screaming and yelling was to be diminished by an increased opacity in the mere name of transparency and efficiency, so that the public could not see whether laws were abided by without making tedious and expensive public record requests. The old administration under Jorge Gonzalez deserved criticism, but it was notably helpful in bending over backwards to supply information free of charge to interested parties, even when that information was not flattering.

If permit decals were not required, the public may not see if signs are permitted. If parking permits are not displayed in vehicles, the public may not see if cars are illegally parked. If the public may no longer access the building permit record online, and must have permission from property owners to see the permits or make a property-by-property public record request, the public cannot check for permits and report violations, nor can delators generally search the records for patterns of violation and possible corruption.

If permit fixers like Permit Doctor are not required to be licensed as are other construction trades, and to register on every permit fixed, the public may not see to what extent permits are properly "expedited."

For instance, I know of one case where a businessman applied for a permit for a parking lot and for several months was frustrated, so he visited Permit Doctor and paid about $1,800. Permit Doctor took a parking lot plan that had been approved for another business out of its filed, carried it next door along with a large colada, and the permit was immediately approved. The gentleman was curious as to what was in that colada.

Another fixer who did a large business in the city and maintained an office here actually signed off on plans as an architect although he was not licensed. He was eventually exposed, after telling an unlicensed contractor doing millions of dollars of business in the city with the knowledge of the Building Department that he was buying a gun "to take care of the reporter," and moved on to another business involving bundles of cash.

As you know, Permit Doctor represents the largest developers and contractors, and efforts therefore to regulate permit fixers as suggested by your predecessor were in vain due to the influence of the real estate industry. The owner rents space at City Hall and many people think Permit Doctor is a branch of the local government.

The sight of all the Permit Doctor signs around town now on big projects gave me cause to wonder as usual if those signs were permitted, or are indicative, under the Broken Windows Theory, that Permit Doctor has ignored codes far more important than the signage code.\It is with that in mind that I ask you whether or not Permit Doctor signs are required to bear permit decals, and if not, why not.

Sincerely,

David Arthur Walters

Cc. Mayor and City Commission

Death Wish South Beach

"I'm going to end up getting killed out here," ended the January 9 *Miami New Times* report everyone is talking about, quoting South Beach vigilante Michael DeFelippi, an erstwhile "plastic bag crusader" who reportedly devotes twenty hours a week now to ridding the decadent beach of its human detritus instead of plastic bags and Styrofoam.

Indeed, if Freud's dual-drive notion derived from his patient Sabina Spielrein, of a death instinct in opposition to an erotic drive, holds true, he may soon take a bullet in the head or a shiv in the back as he stars in his own version of *Death Wish*. That would be a shame because he is a nice guy trying to do good because he that ignores evil is good for nothing.

Although he does not have a real-life superhero moniker and costume, every repeat offender lurking on the beach knows him well for getting them busted on one misdemeanor or not.

No doubt he had better invest several hours a week in martial arts studies. Real-live superhero "Dark Guardian", who challenges pimps, drugsters, and gangsters in New York, is a martial arts instructor. Another martial arts expert who calls himself "Phoenix Jones" patrols Seattle donned in a bulletproof vest and ski mask, occasionally intervening in public assaults. "Captain Oyster" in Queens prefers to address late night crimes with "intellectual discourse," but can also be intimidating.

Martial arts, however, may not save the day. I recall that a martial arts instructor with a black belt was killed in Manhattan when he intervened in a mugging. Ideally, a peacekeeper should be a well-trained cop with ample backup and a gun. Vigilantes arise when police are unable or unwilling to keep the peace.

Another South Beach gentleman with time on his hands, a retired television reporter by the name of John Deutzman, informed *New Times* that he accidentally got DeFelippi involved in the crusade to rid famed Ocean Drive of undesirable habitués, and that DeFelippi loves it so much he should be a cop. According to the *New Times* report, DeFelippi even asked a reporter, "Aren't I a good police officer" after he got cops to chase poor black drug users down an alley. However, he informed me that he never said that, that it was actually pronounced by a police officer, not him. In any event, he *should be* a cop. That is, if the police power works as it should, which was not the case on Ocean Drive, where innocent people became increasingly likely to be robbed or raped after a change in political regimes.

Under the new regime, led by Mayor Phil Levine, a wealthy media mogul and developer who used his fortune to obtain a majority on the city commission thus rendering himself a strong mayor of a city with a weak mayor/strong city manager charter, the South Beach parks began filling up with vagrants. An outsider police chief, Dan Oates, famous for his handling of the Colorado movie shootings, had been hired, and he and the new city manager, Jimmy Morales, former city attorney for the scandalized City of Doral, along with the majority of city commissioners, were said to be subservient to Levine for a spell. Police brass who had been making headway at reforms after the most recent corruption scandal were forced out and replaced.

I was informed by private security guards that they were told by police officers not to disturb indigents in the parks because "parks are their home." A police source informed me that the chief had, on the one hand, made some welcome organization changes, but he was "too liberal," and was having difficulty getting things done his way.

In February of 2017 Mitch Novick, who owns a hotel on Ocean Drive, said: "In my nearly thirty years in the hotel business, I've never seen so many shootings, stabbings, brutal attacks, murders, robberies, sexual assaults, hit and runs, drive-by shootings on Miami Beach. I attribute it entirely to the perpetual carnival-like, crime-ridden circus of Ocean Drive which city commissioners senselessly allow to continue."

Most of the felonies he speaks about were not generated by vagrants and derelicts but by punks from the Mainland.

David Wallach, who owns Mango's Tropical Café on Ocean Drive, drew the ire of former mayor Phil Levine for publicly insisting that the police were not pro-actively enforcing the laws.

Liberal policing may be faulted to a certain extent, but increased traffic since the end of the Great Recession should share the blame. South Beach had already become well known as a hip hop party town with clubs featuring violent rapping on Washington Avenue. "Get your gun, we're going to South Beach," was the refrain.

The inordinately vain mayor, who urged in vain that liquor sales be rolled back from 5 am to 2 am, was even accused by his critics, whom he designated as "screamers and yellers" who would have to wait until the next election to be heard, of doing his best to ghettoize Ocean Drive and Washington Avenue so his developer friends and contributors could gentrify the area.

Voters managed to get the alcohol question he championed on the ballot, and then defeated it as money poured in from the industry with the claim that cutting three hours every night from sales would bankrupt the city and ruin the allure of South Beach. Levine, whose antics had exposed his true colors, decided not to run for another term, and to use his millions to vie for the governor's office. Candidates for the commission sold their souls as usual and came out against the rollback. Protestors who seldom if ever visit Ocean Drive at night marched on the streets against it. Those for the proposal had scant funds for the fight so the question failed.

Business goes on as usual. Current anecdotal reviews of Ocean Drive range from, the police have cleaned up the area, to a few police are around loafing, chatting and fiddling with their cell phones. People who claim to be in the know say not to worry: there are lots of plainclothes cops around. Maybe there are fewer homeless lounging in the park.

In any event, it appears that the heroic vigilantes did not harass the usual suspects including the homeless crowd in vain.

Most real-life superheroes temper their anti-crime crusades with charitable campaigns to help homeless people and hapless minorities. "Blonde" Deutzman and "Crusader" DeFelippi, however, have naturally been cast by civil rights advocates as inimical to the homeless, and the minorities, meaning, on Miami Beach, black people.

Deutzman, incidentally, does not like being called a "vigilante." DeFelippi said he has doubts about the term. Members claim their group is merely a watch group. The "vigil" in "vigilante" means to be awake, i.e. to be alert or *watchful.* Vigilantes are people who appoint themselves or organize themselves with others into unofficial groups to protect their communities by catching and punishing criminals. The two leaders do more than observe and report. They certainly are not a Bernhard Goetz, who shot muggers in an apparent subway sting, and a Rodrigo Duerte, who has admitted to personally murdering drug dealers in the Philippines. Still Deutzman and DeFelippi in their heroic endeavor are obsessive-compulsive, going out on aggressive patrols, squawking at misdemeanor violations, even noisy tour busses, following apparently homeless suspects and others around and recording them, making sure they are frisked and punished by legal authorities.

Deutzman informed me that "those who declare themselves 'homeless' are responsible for thirty-percent of the arrests in town. The police," he said, "put 'homeless' on the arrest form, a legal sworn document, just because the defendant tells them so. No proof is needed. That gets sympathy from the system, whether it's true or not. And here's the big thing: It's not illegal to be homeless, but on Miami Beach it's illegal to sleep in any public park after midnight. So it kind of is illegal to be homeless."

He went to bond court, where most cases are disposed of, to call to the court's attention the long records of the repeat offenders in hopes they will be kept off the streets with jail sentences. He pointed out to me that there is plenty of room in the jails, so that should be no excuse for releasing them so they can come right back to South Beach ton prey on residents and tourists.

He said he has spent hundreds of dollars out of his own pocket compiling relevant crime statistics from the public records. He said that "98.3 percent of all misdemeanors were pled out or disposed of in Bond Court in 2016. We are trying to break the cycle of 1-day sentences for all misdemeanors. In 2016 only 59 such cases were sentenced." Amazingly, one offender had been arrested 343 times.

He cited the record of an alleged rapist as an example of judicial negligence: "Prior to his horrifying alleged rape of an innocent tourist, the documented lawlessness and violent behavior of Derrick Keith Wiggins should have set off alarms and raised red flags way before his heinous act. Records show he had strong warning signs of a sexual predator with recent alarming crimes involving female victims, including attempted kidnapping, recent batteries, indecent exposure, lewd and lascivious and the usual laundry list of crimes that go relatively unpunished. The alleged rape was his 10th arrest this year, his 22nd since March of 2015. Most puzzling is that Wiggins was just released on his own recognizance as a homeless person without an address three days before the alleged rape."

All he wants, Deutzman told me, is to have the "bad guys," which he characterized as "super bacteria," removed from Lummus Park. "It's absurd that we can't control the park."

There has been plenty of derogatory macho talk among the vigilante group led by DeFelippi and Deutzman, his appointed Facebook "monitor" Immediately after his appointment, Deutzman proceeded to post his own opinions and to dispute objections, at one time insisting that people should just trust him to lead, as if he were the ultimate authority on the subject, which at one time happened to be the necessity of removing public park benches. He said that only people with 50 arrests sat on those benches.

Curiously, the former television journalist now vigilante group monitor proceeded to kick members out of the group's secret virtual clubhouse hosted by Facebook if they got "off message," such as the homeless advocate who disagreed with the monitor. I myself was booted.

I had stated that police methods had changed since I lived on the beach off and on since 1970, and that the misbehavior we see now is said to be the "cost of freedom," and that freedom had really increased on Ocean Drive and the parks since the installation of the new regime, namely its current mayor, city manager, and police chief. I said nothing intentionally insulting towards anyone and was on-topic.

Deutzman intervened to dispute with me, misinterpreting what I had said, and addressing me by the wrong name, and bragged about his media experience and his study of the problem for one year.

In fact, both he and DeFelippi are relative newcomers to South Beach. I stated that I had lived and studied the problem for decades, and that people are ignorant who think certain park benches were made for criminals instead of law abiding people, so that the benches must be removed instead of the criminals. I said the problem is really a dysfunctional government.

I was about to post some links to my own coverage of the subject only to discover that Monitor Deutzman had evicted me from the vigilante Facebook feed, so I messaged him and asked him for an apology along with my reinstatement and reposting of my commentary.

I said that his knee-jerk eviction reminded me of my studies of the formation of the Ku Klux Klan, the Nazi party, and France's notorious Committee of Public Safety.

He ordered me not to "go there" because, he said, his grandfather had been a cop who fought the Klan. But I wondered why that should exempt his own behavior from criticism.

He said I had to abide by his rules and that those rules were common to monitoring. That was indeed a false statement, I remarked, because he had not behaved like a monitor but like a dictator over the content of the discussion. He said discussions must be on his track, and that I should go to other groups. And then he said he had actually ejected me from the vigilantes because I had insulted him, and that no one had ever spoken to him as I had done.

I messaged DeFelippi about the behavior of his monitor. He responded that the discussions of his vigilantes must be nonpolitical. I responded that politics is about the distribution of power, and that it is legitimate and necessary to criticize the exercise of that power. After all, the police department is a hierarchical command organization; cops are not inclined to run around and do their own thing unless badly managed; orders come from the top down; the chief at the top is under a political thumb.

I yet again asked vainly for an apology and the retraction of the accusation that my behavior was immoral or insulting prior to my eviction from the vigilante committee unless someone chose to be insulted.

Deutzman offered to take me back into the group, as he has done with the homeless advocate he kicked out of the group several times. I declined upon reconsideration because the secrecy of group implied I would have a conflict of interest as a journalist for actually participating in its affairs instead of spying on it to reveal its secrets.

Secret societies have their virtues as may be apparent from the fact that several United States Presidents have belonged to them, but vigilante societies can be vicious. Secret Facebook groups have dedicated themselves to laudable endeavors, but secrecy can be conducive to criminal behavior, such as the secret Facebook group that was infiltrated by Chicago police and busted for trafficking in guns and dope.

DeFelippi and his group were recently lauded by no less than billionaire Mark Zuckerberg. At a meeting with only 19 selected interest group administrators in Silicon Valley celebrating *FB 13th Birthday,* he said groups like DeFelippi's have the capacity to heal widening divisions everywhere in the world. He told DeFelippi that the world needs to gather to build his kind of community.

That kind of community, a *secret* community, however, may contribute to further divisiveness, as was mentioned recently by former President Barrack Obama, who objected to the "balkanization" of social media. In fact, that controversy is nothing new. The Founding Fathers warned against "factions." Yet eventually political factions hewing to divisive ideologies instead of practical behavior won black-versus-white thinkers over, and then interest group politics further limited the possibility of a sane, wholesome body politic.

The hostile rhetoric of the DeFelippi/Deutzman vigilante group goes farther than characterizing undesirable humans as subhuman "super bacteria." In an exchange about stings, DeFelippi reportedly said he would love to entrap a scumbag, to which someone added a remark razor blades should cut them up. The chief said civilian stings are inappropriate. DeFelippi, when he was reprimanded by police officers for his tactics, reportedly said he wished he could come around with a paintball gun and "(expletive deleted) nail' the drug dealers. Deutzman made a remark that the bridges to South Beach should be dynamited. After DeFelippi was reprimanded by police officers for his tactics, he reportedly said he wished he could come around with a paintball and "(Expletive deleted) nail" the drug dealers.

The South Beach vigilantes believe denigrating and hostile language is just kidding around. Interestingly, Charles Bronson, when interviewed about being cast in *Death Wish,* said he was not kidding when he said he would like to shoot criminals. No doubt his audience shared the sentiment. Everyone with a conscience has an inner cop, and some of those cops would like to take justice into their own hands just as some real cops actually do. Many people are would-be vigilantes, and that is why vigilante movies have a great box office.

Inept government is at the root of vigilantism. South Beach residents are sick and tired of being overruled by politicians who prostitute themselves to a tourist industry that may complain about policing but objects to rolling back liquor sale hours, lobbies again tax increases, yet does little to privately secure the safety of law-abiding people from predators, such as provide its own vigilant security patrols.

No matter who is elected, it is business as usual. The overwhelming, F-type majority follows suit. It is the failure of the police department that gives people cause to imagine harming criminals, and they might actually shoot them if they would not be arrested for doing so.

However that may be, tourists from afar are becoming increasingly aware of the "super bacteria" as well as the Zika virus on Miami Beach, and that, along with exorbitant rents and outrageous prices for services rendered by lowly paid and often rude employees, is taking its toll in paradise.

Former commissioner and prosecutor Michael Grieco, whose candidacy for mayor and then re-election as commissioner was brought to naught on a trumped-up criminal charge involving the contribution of a foreigner to a political action committee, remarked that the petty criminals can do almost anything they want in Miami Beach because the judicial system is a frustrating turnstile.

Hope springs eternal. Residents hope Grieco's opponent and winner of the mayor's office, Dan Gelber, a former corruption prosecutor, called "Pious Dan" for his Talmudic disposition and recitation of the Decalogue's injunction against covetousness, shall lead Miami Beach closer to Zion, a place where all will be welcome according to messianic authorities. Nevertheless, Cynics have good reason to believe Solomon was right when he said there shall be nothing new under the Sun.

Grieco has recently formed a Facebook group call HUB. Someone posted a report on its news feed along with a photo stating that police officers were sitting on their ATVs in Lummus Park talking on their cell phones as usual. I commented that I had been evicted from the vigilante Facebook group for criticizing policing in the park, but still had given the secret group credit for its efforts. A HUB member immediately criticized me for making the critical remark, said the vigilante group was not a vigilante group, but is a watch group, and asked who are we going to rely on if not the police officers.

Of course we will rely on their replacements if they do not do their job. It remains to be seen if the replacement of the leadership will do any good inasmuch as we are discussing the same problems for decades. We still have high hopes for Michael Grieco because he understood why two good citizens took it upon themselves to be vigilantes, so-called, and, as commissioner, he contradicted Mayor Levine, who originally backed him.

Grieco's HUB group went secret so I bowed out to avoid a conflict of interest from active participation. I asked him why he made his group secret.

"On January 1 of this year we launched the Miami Beach "Hub" in which ideas and information can be shared with a focus on problem-solving and accuracy. A troll-free Facebook group where verified Miami Beach residents/workers/business owners can sound off safely and connect with other groups, pages etc. It's a work in progress but clearly we are filling a void in that over 1,500 locals have joined in just over two weeks. We are trying to promote active civic engagement and community. We made it 'secret' but that sounds more important than reality. That setting simply prevents unsolicited membership requests and means it no longer pops up in searches. There are a half-dozen moderators in addition to myself."

Michael Grieco is of course a friend of Michael DeFelippi, and I consider the both of them as friends with whom I may have friendly disagreements. I was concerned by DeFelippi's statement that he would wind up being killed.

The older I get the more I believe in law and order. A police state would suit me providing the laws were equitable and evenly enforced. Still, I have my reservations from my rebellious youth, and I worry that this vigilantism business, which I am myself engaged in as a self-appointed muckraker, is a dangerous form of neurosis in the retaliatory Miami Beach culture. Wherefore I recommended a homeopathic remedy to temper our obsessive-compulsive fault-finding.

"Michael," I said, under an email headed *We Are Neurotic*, "I think we exhibit the same sort of neurotic behavior and may go stark raving mad or come to a bad end without therapy. I suggest we get together, get drunk, smoke dope, and spend the evening with a whore, two if we can afford it. What do you think?"

I have no response to date. I fear he may be taking my suggestion too seriously.

Perhaps we can all have a drink and watch the exotic dancers at Mangos. I asked owner David Wallach to what extent he attributes the criminal issues on Ocean Drive to a deficit in policing. "How are things going now, and why?"

He evaded a direct answer with, "Take a walk, or ride, any day of the week from 5th Street to 15 Street at any hour, all day and all night. Concentrate on all daylight hours and dinner through 10:30 pm, and then do it later and into the late hours. Do that multiple days. Check especially on the West sidewalk where thousands of people walk. Please let me know what you see or don't see."

I must leave that to the vigilante group for now. He neglected to recommend a drink at his place while ogling his dancing beauties. I had two fingers of scotch over the last year and got a headache. Maybe a tropical rum drink would serve the purpose this year.

Subsequent Note: Deutzman moved to Waikiki where he surfs in the morning. Mayor Gelber has managed to run the South Beach Entertainment District into the ground pursuant to Levine's plan with developers to turn it into a nice office and Art Deco district with a kiddie park and Ferris wheel. 16 October 2021

The South Beach Man Who Almost Lives in His Car

Why would a man who has a home live in his car?

Leroy, who happens to be a black man in his forties, would not give me his real name. He virtually lived in his dilapidated compact car near the corner of Euclid Avenue and 6th Street before the cops made him move it. I say 'virtually' because he claims he does not really live in the car. We have seen him living in it for over a year in the old South Beach neighborhood called Seventh Heaven – the gangsta rap nightclub and crime-ridden neighborhood between 7th and 5th Streets. The Flamingo Park Neighborhood, a much better neighborhood to the north, adopted the old crack-hood without its permission, but you would never know it.

Now Seventh Heaven is sometimes referred to as The Toilet or The Capitol of Poop due to the piles of dog feces, some of it deposited directly in the middle of sidewalks, a tribute to the rapidly spreading culture of disrespect aided by a lack of good enforcement and appropriate legislation. Not to mention, by the way, the alley and parking lot near the nightclubs, sometimes so full of human feces and stinking urine that passersby cross the street holding their noses.

A few yuppies moved into the predominantly Hispanic hood following a hopeful attempt at gentrification by property owners. But it is difficult to fight the blight, and the recent condominium conversions suffer an encroachment aggravated by the Great Recession. A large number of people whom Hispanics call gentuza reside in the crime-ridden hood. Many of the Hispanics are hard-working, hard-drinking, paperless men. Yet we have suffered the arrival of a relatively more violent contingent, from Guatemala, which has a high rate of violence against women – one man in our neighborhood, wanted in Guatemala for murder, stabbed his wife seventeen times. Another woman was stabbed in the neck one morning on Meridian Avenue – the paper reported she was not a tourist, so city hall breathed a sigh of relief. Another woman was dragged down the alley and knifed and raped behind the Meridian Market in the wee hours – a yuppie neighbor said she was not surprised that a woman out alone so late on foot would suffer such consequences. You get the picture. And we have low-level drug dealers, and a smattering of old-timers who fled Cuba, many of them on some sort of dole. White trash is sparse, and there are only a handful of American blacks.

Mind you that Seventh Heaven, call it The Toilet if you will, is paradise in comparison to many other city neighborhoods in the world, so you will pay around $800 a month for your room – a Puerto Rican man and his wife, two babies, stepmother and a dog lived in one studio for three years until he managed to find a big subsidized place for his family in North Beach. A tourist might find the area quite attractive, and would love living in it until she found out where she was.

The refuse that Leroy left on the curb – empty take-out bags, cans and bottles, some of them full of urine, a spare tire – certainly did not detract from the hood's bad reputation. He was a pathetic sight when sleeping in his little compact car. You could not see him on a cool night because he covered up the windows with paper and cardboard, but he had to roll them down when the weather was hot and humid lest he suffocate, and there he was, for all to see and pity, hunched up and sweating in the front seat, his back seat jammed with gear and rubbish.

'Uhma', a crack whore and sometime drug dealer from Pakistan, pitied Leroy the most and served him food at the curb. Uhma liked to say that every man has a penis, but that she cares only for the men who have the 'bump' she loves (crack), so she partied with almost every man in her apartment building, depending on who had the supplies, besides the Italian drug dealer she lived with and dealt drugs for at the front desk of the hotel where she worked. Well, a Samoan once told me that you know when it's time to divorce your wife when you have your organ in one hand your money in the other and she takes the money.

Uhma got pregnant, lost the child, and then the hood got hot with cops, so she moved away with her most significant other, leaving Leroy a bit in the lurch. Yes, she had a soft spot for Leroy, even though he had no bump to speak of. To give her credit for such charity, Uhma might have been a good girl if she had not left her father in Pakistan. In any event, Leroy liked her cooking, and left the paper plates and plastic utensils on the curb with the rest of the trash.

Almost every morning, Leroy was also seen and heard at the local homeless burger joint, the Burger King on 5th Street and Alton Road. By that time he had cleaned himself up and changed into nice clothes. He was heard well and at length by everyone who showed up for breakfast. He talked loudly and ceaselessly at the two homeless lesbians who breakfasted for two or three hours every morning at Burger King. He often ventured with them to the little library in the upscale South Pointe neighborhood. The lesbian pair, perhaps his only friends, manage to listen to his blathering intently. They are of his color but somewhat lighter. Both are terribly obese. They dress like gypsies and go about with lots of gear, their worldly possessions. They love to use the computers for hours on end – the librarian gives them extra time. Nobody is bothered by them there, except occasionally by the couple's odor; and once an East European man complained about the scene frequently displayed on their computer monitors – depictions of breast operations.

Now Leroy had himself a residential parking permit for his jalopy, which he occasionally moved a space or two nearer the corner where Las Olas Café is located. He kept his beat-up bicycle, his real transportation, chained to a tree near his car. We figured he was on the dole, got food stamps, maybe disability payments, sold some dope somewhere, whatever. Survival is the goal, and some people are more ingenious at it than others. For example, a Cuban-American gay couple, one of whom is an expert at conning people out of money, had four jobs at the height of the tourist season. They were taking in up to $5,000 tax free in a month, putting the funds on cash cards since they do not want bank accounts. They enjoyed almost fully subsidized housing among other social benefits.

Despite our neighborhood's reputation, many of my neighbors complained to the Miami Beach Code Compliance Division and Police Department about the man who lived in his car. But they were told that there is nothing that could be done about him unless he was seen committing some crime.

I felt a little sorry for Leroy because I was homeless several times in my youth, some time before it was politically correct to feel very sorry for homeless people, and I was amused by Leroy's cheap rent, the small fee he paid for his monthly parking permit. It was only after he was observed selling residential parking permits to tourists that I decided lodge a complaint myself. I stopped two Parking Enforcement officers and informed them of the illegal sale of parking permits. Everybody knew Leroy was living in his car there, including Sanitation and Parking. I figured Leroy was getting blank temporary or monthly permits from friends in Parking. I was incensed by the possibility of public corruption; otherwise I would not have complained. Nothing was done.

As fate would have it, Leroy was getting out of his car one morning, half-dressed, stretching out his limbs, right across the street from Las Olas Café, when the July 2010 Las Olas Conference was in session. Gathered there were representatives from the City Manager's Office, the Police Department, the Miami Beach Community Development Corporation, and the Code Compliance Division. I was the sole representative of the Public because of inadequate public notice, and they were sorry I showed up. The officials were there to pat themselves on the back for what a good job they were doing and then to walk around the neighborhood. Whenever I tried to make a constructive suggestion or to present evidence contrary to the positive mental attitude affirmations being made, the officials tried unsuccessfully to shut me up. Finally, they gave up, got up and left without doing a Potemkin walkabout.

At one point, the City Manager's representative who coordinated the Conference was shushing me when I tried to object to the claim that city officials were doing a great job enforcing the Code in my hood. I objected, and said that she and the city manager are the ones who should shut up and listen, and take a good look at the violations.

"Look, look right behind you, at the man who lives in his car," I said. "He leaves rubbish on the curb, and sells parking permits, and he's been there for a year or more."

Detectives showed up across the street immediately, flashed their badges and questioned Leroy. In less than ten minutes, Leroy and his car were gone. Apparently, the police representative at the Conference had waved her magic Blackberry, or detectives were cruising the area during the Conference.

I encountered Leroy a few days later and identified myself as a reporter.

"I saw the cops swoop in on you the other day, and then you and your car disappeared. It was your unlucky day. There was a meeting of cops and officials across the street going on when you got out of your car half-dressed. What happened to you?"

"The police made me move to another area," he said. "They asked me for my identification but not my registration. I was getting dressed from my trunk, and they were looking for drugs."

"Do you sell drugs?"

"Hell, no. The cops know me. There were undercover drug cops all over the neighborhood at night, and they didn't bother me."

"You said 'were' – have the undercovers left the neighborhood?"

"Yeah, they moved over to Michigan Avenue. There used to be drugs dealers all over Euclid, but they arrested some of them, and some moved. They know I don't sell drugs. But when I go to the beach, tourists come up and ask me for drugs all the time."

"Why?"

"Because I'm black, that's why, and I look homeless. Tourists can get anything they want from the homeless who hang out in the park by the beach. The narcotics detectives should take care of that, get to their suppliers."

"So you had to move your car?"

"I didn't have to – I have a permit to park anywhere in a residential area I want to. But I moved the car anyway."

"So you live in your car. Is it legal to live in a car in the city limits?"

"I don't really live there. I have an apartment."

"Huh?"

"I have a place to live."

"Why don't you live there?"

"I do. But I don't get along with my girlfriend. She's Cuban. She doesn't speak English and I don't speak Spanish, and she won't teach me Spanish."

"Maybe if you could communicate you would hate each other," I reflected, thinking about the Hispanic woman who learned English and found out her American boyfriend was the kind of man she did not like let alone love.

"She stays there. It's my home. I take care of hygiene there," he said, showing me his keys.

"I thought you were homeless, or that your car was your home."

"No, I don't live in my car, because I have a home. I just go to my car sometimes."

"I see you there a lot, sometimes every night."

"I'm trying to get back in the workforce now. I got a part-time job with the County. I have a Class A license. I can drive trucks, you know. "

"Good. You were observed selling residential parking permits. Where did you get them?"

"Oh, they were mine, I get them."

"From whom do you get them?"

Leroy would not answer, and started to move away.

"It's the valets who make money off tourists, sixty to ninety dollars a night, with those permits," he said over his shoulder.

"You had a bicycle by your car."

"It was stolen."

"What's your name?"

He shook his head negatively, and hurried away.

"Okay, I'll call you Leroy," I yelled after him.

His story reminded me of the time my latest wife got fed up with me because the expenses of my Mark IV Lincoln Continental exceeded the house payments. She said my brown-capped white coupe looked like a phallus, and ordered me to drive it down to the beach and live in it. I eventually would up living in a swank oceanfront condo with a Swedish masseuse. I was not about to live in my car! In fact, I eventually took my ex-wife's advice - I no longer have a car. I don't envy Leroy at all.

South Beach Rigga Rap

I had never heard the word "wigga" until Doc Hanley pronounced it in the car after he saved me from Ft. Lauderdale. I had landed there two days before Hurricane Jeanne blew in. My hotel reservation had been deleted because I was illegally bumped for someone willing to pay a higher rate. A cab driver took me to a decrepit motel, in what is euphemistically called the "inner city," where I was able to rent one of the last rooms available.

It was an interesting place. Russian "exchange students" posing as maids were the center of attraction, especially when they swam nude in the scum-laden pool as the storm whipped up. The lights went out, and people from the hood surrounding the motel were knocking on the doors, asking for money, cigarettes, food, whatever could be spared.

So Doc, a veteran SEAL, bailed me out after the eye of the hurricane passed by. I asked him what in the world a "wigga" meant as we waited in line at a gas station. He pointed out a white man who was vacuuming out his car as rap music blared from inside the car, rattling the vehicle as if it were a tin can. The man had his pants pulled way down in back, showing black boxers with big pink polka dots.

"That's a wigga," he said.

"What?"

"A white nigga."

"Oh."

I had never heard of such a thing. I was a small town "inner city" guy myself. That would be Topeka ("a good place to grow potatoes"). I ran with the Mexicans from the other side of the tracks back then. My good friend, a black kid named Clifford Taylor, with whom I liked to wrestle, lived across the street. My very best friend was Jim Norton, a Mormon boy who wound up having two wives. The worst trouble Clifford, Jim and I got in was for peeing in the finger paint pots at school.

I had the run of Topeka. I liked to visit Roy, an older black fellow who lived near the Capitol. He and his wife drank orange juice and whisky with breakfast on Sundays. I did not know any racists, but I guess there was plenty of racism in Topeka because sometimes I saw groups of black people marching around the neighborhood near Topeka High School singing "We Shall Overcome," and I heard something about a Board of Education case that had the word "brown" in it.

Long story short, I eventually ran away to Chicago when I was thirteen, where a black cook took me in and saved me from starving. He had a dozen white boys in his South Side crib. He turned out to be a pederast, so I hit the streets again. Fortunately I was taken in by a gay couple who kept their hands off me, and they kept me supplied with food and vodka and orange juice. I got a job, and then my very own crummy room in a Puerto Rican neighborhood. I eventually moved on to Manhattan. There were so many black people around my "inner city" "salt and pepper" hoods that I did not think in black and white, but rather in blurry terms.

The blacks called me "grey boy." They were more or less sophisticated, though some were pimps and drug dealers. I asked one of them about the "N-word" the rappers were using, why black people would use that word if it was demeaning, something whites put on them.

"New York blacks are not niggers," said one city slicker. "Niggers are ignorant Southern blacks."

"Niggers can call each other niggers," another said, "and throw it back with pride at white people, but coming from whites it is an insult."

I was not even inclined to use the so-called N-word. I did enjoy it mouthed by Ice-T when he got popular. Rappers I noticed liked to use the "B-word," which I thought was insulting to females in general unless they were the ones using it.

Well, Miami, as everyone knows, is notorious for racism. I saw the riots on TV years ago. And I had lived in South Beach in the late Sixties, where I learned that blacks must be off the beach at sundown or else. Things have changed. Not many blacks live on the beach, but they like to come over from the Mainland and hang out. And thousands swarm to the beach for Memorial Day and Spring Break. The troublemakers among them are mostly from South Florida.

I thought of Doc, may he rest in peace, when I passed by a Washington Avenue tattoo parlor shortly after I arrived. A heavily tattooed white man, with pants pulled down, and a black fellow sporting lots of bling, were chatting by the doorway. During the course of their exchange, wherein every fifth word was the F-word, the black man addressed the white guy as "nigga" several times, and I noticed that when he did so the white guy's face lit up with delight.

"Wow," I thought, "that is what Doc was talking about. The fellow is a wigga for sure. And the black man is playing him."

Now I do not like to use vulgar language unless I am really angry and lose control, and even then I do not use racist terms as I was not raised early on in that climate. Still I believed the meaning of wigga should be memorialized, so I put on my Nicki Minaj album yesterday and jotted down the following:

South Beach Wigga Rap

Sample Lyric by Grey Boy

SCENE:

Chorus and Wigga in front of Washington Avenue tattoo parlor, Duck Tours bus passing by, Wigga has pants way down and has big slice of pizza

CHORUS:

Hey, hey, looka you, looka you
White boy, wigga now, wigga now,
You a South Beach wigga boy now,
Wigga bona fide boy,
What you say now (what you say now)

WIGGA:

I say fuckada fuck!
I'm a fuckin South Beach wigga!
Looka me now South Beach Duck Tours,
Go fuck a duck, I'm a wigga now,
Fucka ducka fucka ducka

CHORUS:
Hey, hey, looka you, looka you
White boy nigga now, wigga now,
You a South Beach wigga boy now,
Wigga nigga bona fide boy,
What you say now (what you say now)
WIGGA:
I ain't afraid (I ain't afraid)
I got my piece (I got my piece)
I got my slice (I got my slice)
I'm a wigga (I'm a wigga)
I'm a fuckin South Beach wigga
I'm a pants down wigga nigga,
On the fuckin beach with bitches
Grabbin my crotch (grabbin my crotch)
Saying fuckety fuckety fuck,
I've got it made (I've got it made)
I ain't afraid (I ain't afraid)
I got my slice, I got my piece,
I got bitches, I got bitches,
They got their tits I got my tats,
Fuckin white boys go fuck yourselves
I got it all, I got it all,
I'm the man now, I'm the man now,
Fucka ducka fuckety fuck
I'm a wigga, I'm a wigga
CHORUS:
Hey, hey, looka you, looka you
White boy, nigga now, wigga now,
You a South Beach wigga boy,
Wigga nigga bona fide boy
You a nigga toy, wigga boy!

Pleasure Emporium Burnt to Cinders

The building at 1019 5th Street occupied by Pleasure Emporium, which was gutted by a mysterious fire starting in the roof over the front door, is now for sale as made evident by two signs placed on the building by real estate agent Jonathan Eisman of Lombardi Properties.

Code Compliance administrator George Castell said he was sending an officer to the scene to investigate the fact that the two signs do not have $25 sign permit decals on them as required by local ordinances.

As for the fire, rumors were afloat in the neighborhood that it was ignited by one Juanita Emporia Placer, a disgruntled S&M model whose body was allegedly found in the building by firefighters. A source who did not want to be identified because he is married said Placer was a former nun featured in Craig A. Monson's book, Nuns Behaving Badly: Tales of Music, Magic, Art, and Arson in the Convents, on sale at the store.

Miami Beach firefighters are to be commended for their heroic efforts to save what appeared to be a scantily clad woman from the fire. However, according to South Beach Police Commander Captain Enrique Doce, the body found under a rack was actually a mannequin.

The fire was apparently not intentionally set by a disgruntled member of South Beach's once booming sex industry—Walgreen's condom sales on 5th Street set a national store record in 2012. A copy of the fire report is expected to be received by in seven or eight months if the editor can raise $3,400 for the public record request.

Customers unaware of the fire, none of whom would speak on the record, have been trickling to the shop ever since. The owners of the Pleasure Emporium business reported on their website that they were unsure of whether they would reopen the store.

Naughty Rooster Arises From Pleasure Emporium

The prurient spirit of Pleasure Emporium, a South Beach sex paraphernalia boutique at 1019 Fifth Street that burnt to cinders in July 2014, has arisen in 2019 as the Naughty Rooster, replacing the interim tenant, Mattress One, a firm sometimes known for ridges, lumps and bumps, sinking feelings, and flying by night.

Naughty Rooster also inserted itself into the Pleasure Emporium location at 1671 Alton Road, but the pleasuring outfit did not take to the mattresses there before a conversion into a cocky rooster. It went flaccid and closed amid the renovation orgy along that side of the Alton block.

A Pleasure Emporium in Hollywood, Florida, was notably scandalized by the media in 2018. Broward County Judge Ginger Lerner-Wren dismissed charges bought against numerous gentlemen arrested for lewd and lascivious conduct, or, to put it nicely, engaging in consensual relations in private booths. One badly acting gentleman was fired from his job over the erotic publicity, which was replete with shaming mugshots. The Constitution was constructively stretched by caviling pundits to imply that oral sex is a form of free speech. In any case, the judge ruled that private is private is private hence is none of the public's damn business.

The presiding officer of Naughty Rooster, one 'Martin' whose surname appears as 'Haid,' 'Hadel', and 'Hadle' in official documents, is apparently an investor associated with multiple businesses, such as Horse Hung, Hung Films, SeXXXy Lady, Rooster's Coop, Factory Outlet, and Condenser People. He may be reached in a private rented box at a UPS store in Miami Beach, or at a refrigerator coil cleaning company in an industrial complex in Des Plaines, Illinois. A 'Brittany Haid' of Des Plaines also stars on one of the documents.

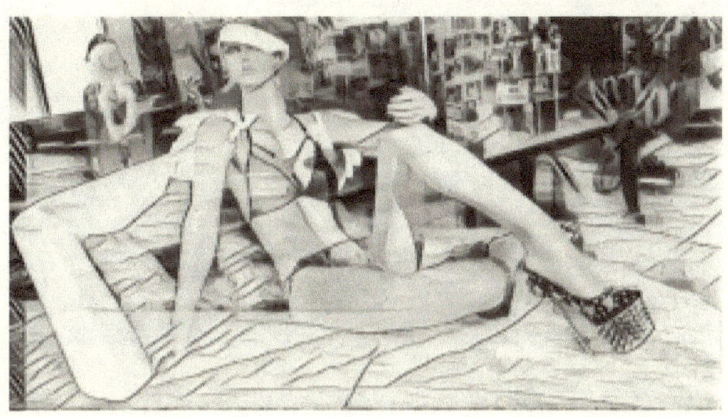

The demand for mattresses is steady in bed-ridden South Beach since mattresses are designed to become uncomfortable for sensitive people in about five years. For a fee on the purchase of a new mattress, the old ones will be taken away by the trucking company to be recycled, or they may be illegally dumped in the alley where poorer residents retrieve them for use for another twenty years, turning them every which way to even out the lumps.

I noticed a sign advertising a coming mattress outlet in the window of 1031 Fifth Street, next door to Naughty Rooster. That parcel is part of 'BLVD at Lenox', a newly completed, four-story structure with 82,000 square feet of retail space.

Michael Comras, a highly regarded commercial broker and developer, assembled four parcels for the complex including that address for a $8.5 million, chump change compared to the $370 million he sold a Lincoln Road block for.

The assembled parcels had been occupied by Carefree Lifestyle, a concierge company that provided gentlemen with nice rides, and a two-story nightclub called IVY, criticised for discriminating in favor of rich gentlemen and beautiful women. IVY was formerly the Club Play.

BLVD is across Lennox Avenue from the 'Fifth and Alton' complex, which stands at the entrance to South Beach at the foot of the MacArthur Causeway. Fifth and Alton is fully occupied by the likes of Ross Stores, Best Buy, Total Wine, and Publix. There are enough parking spaces between the two complexes to park around 1,300 cars.

Developer Russell Galbut is erecting a high rise at the foot of the causeway from Miami, much to the consternation of beleaguered drivers. The area is already densely populated with relatively prosperous people. Here the divide between rich and poor widens remarkably according to the ballad, "the rich get richer and the poor poorer." That is inevitable in a free market, or at least one where entrepreneurs are on the make and politicians on the take. Yes, the market is a bit soft at present given the skyrocketing prices, but whosoever holds out long enough will probably get out more than they put in the international money laundry; that is, notwithstanding another crash, and providing officials withstand the prophesied biblical flood with defensive infrastructure instead of wasting more taxpayer money on frivolities and absurdities.

I asked Mr. Comras about the mattress signage, whether or not Mattress One would move in there. No, he said, that will be another mattress company.

"Targets long anticipated arrival has been well received and provides convenience to Miami Beach residents and visitors. Joining Target is SunTrust Bank, Mattress Firm and a series of yet to be announced retailers and service providers."

Read the reviews on Mattress Firm, including the advertisement by a Doctor of Mattress Comfort certifying to the superior quality of the products. Nevertheless, an independent undercover investigation should be conducted into the mattress business. I hear it can be pretty shady in those little factories that serve big names. We can only hope the mattresses will provide firm support for South Beach's active nightlife, which seems to be on the decline lately along with condom sales.

NOTE: Former S&M model and nun Juanita Emporia Placer, a person of interest in the South Beach Pleasure Emporium fire and several other sex shop fires, is rumored to be at large after fleeing to Italy, and was reportedly last seen at Vatican City.

Mattresses Replace Dildos in South Beach

Update To Old Fast Breaking Sex News Story: The burned out space at 1019 Fifth Street in Miami Beach once occupied by Pleasure Emporium has been repaired and occupied by a Mattress One outlet.

A sex fiend speaking on condition of anonymity said he now purchases his sex accoutrements online. He misses the old store very much, he said, because he liked to mingle with other shoppers there and exchange notes and telephone numbers. He said he had passed by the new store on the way to the Burger King down the street, and noticed the Sealy mattresses.

"Sealy mattresses are great for kinky sex in bed," he said, "but I prefer water beds."

Another gentleman commenting under condition of anonymity related that he had ventured to Pleasure Emporium with his girlfriend because she wanted to buy a dildo.

"As she shopped, I watched an eclectic crowd moving around the store, buying sexy lingerie, sex toys, movies, masks, whips, and other things. I saw two guys come out of the men's room together. The older man, who was wearing a wedding ring, gave the younger one a $50 bill.

"My girlfriend found a great battery-powered dildo. We tried it out that night. She said she would use it a lot when I was out of town on business."

Mattress One is a very large independent Florida and Texas retailer reportedly beneficially owned by Mohanad Salem in Miami-Dade County, and by his relatives elsewhere in Florida.

Mattress scams seem endemic to the retail mattress industry throughout the country. The Better Business Bureau and various authorities received numerous complaints about Mattress One from consumers according to an 18 June 2015 Channel 10 ABC News report by Christina Vazquez, ranging from failure to deliver to a "feeling of falling" when using a mattress. The advertising in the store shows a fully clothed couple sitting comfortably in bed. It is unknown at this time whether any complaints have been made about sexual experiences with the mattresses.

An anonymous source to Vasquez' exposés, a central Florida store manager, said the poor response issues were due to under-staffing of the corporate customer service department, and that the sagging or soft feeling may be the result of the way the mattresses are stacked.

Sagging may occur because the mattresses are used or have used material. A mattress will last perhaps four or five years, regardless of longer warranty periods, and the warranties may apply only if the mattress has sagged two inches. A consumer may pay $1,000 for a supposedly new mattress only to have it sag less than two inches within a month, still giving sleepers the feeling of falling into a hole.

Federal and state laws originally responding to bedbug infestation requires mattresses containing used material to be clearly tagged with that information.

The Florida Attorney General on 15 October 2015 obtained an "Assurance of Voluntary Compliance" with owners and suppliers of Mattress One assuring the state that the prohibitions against unfair and deceptive trade practices would be complied with, including but not limited to selling used sleep items as new or not labeling them as used. Consumers were also assured that what they ordered would be delivered, and that excessive or unfair return fees would not be imposed. The respondents did not admit to anything, but agreed to pay restitution in the amount of $325,000.

Mattress One at the old Pleasure Emporium is conveniently located within blocks of hundreds of luxury condominium apartments. Hopefully a fire sale will not be needed to move the goods.

Fast Breaking Sex Shop Beach News

Sweet Strains in Flamingo Park

I sat down in Flamingo Park today to rest my feet. A woman happened to be playing a saxophone nearby. The sweet strains rested my mind, nearly moving me to tears. I walked over and thanked her.

"Is that tune you are playing was from the repertoire of Duke Ellington? It had a similar swing to it and the same chords as Satin Doll?"

"No, sir, it is not."

"I love the way you play. Are you with a band?"

"No, I play on my own."

"You would make considerable money playing on Lincoln Road, but without a permit, you would be fined."

"I am just practicing. I am not interested in the money. I always bring my instrument with me from Germany when I travel so I can practice."

"I was once quite a good musician on the accordion," I remarked, "but I got tired of lugging it around and eventually pawned it for groceries when I got married."

She smiled at that.

"I like seeing your bicycle with your saxophone and your blonde hair because I have been taking seriously the bikes stolen from a friend of mine, who happens to be of German extract and has blonde hair. Do you know you are responsible for the bike if it is stolen? I don't know why the bike rental companies do not have a blanket policy or offer insurance."

"That is why I carried two locks with me, to lock it to parking furniture. I love riding around South Pointe Park and back."

"That is precisely what my friend Elizabeth loves to do. May I take your picture?"

"Of course, and I shall play Georgia on My Mind because it is a song for you."

Since I had heard her speaking in Spanish with another passerby, I then knew she was fluent in Spanish and English and German. Perhaps she detected a bit of a southern accent in my voice.

"That would be a good song for me, because I went to military school in Gainesville, a short distance from Atlanta, in the beautiful Blue Ridge Mountains. I could sing that song well long ago, but I stopped singing twenty years ago."

Her rendition was lovely.

"Don't go to Lincoln Road," I yelled at her when I walked away after she was finished with my song, "because people will throw money at you there."

"Don't worry," she hollered after me, and I thought I should take up playing a musical instrument again

South Beach B****

A friend of mine speaks of some women in the most vulgar language, especially Melania and Ivanka. He reserves the foulest vulgarities for Ivanka, whom he said tried to cheat him, which I believe because many others who have done business with her in Florida have said the same thing

I refrain from cursing women by reference to their gender, especially their genitals, and I've told him I do not appreciate it, yet he continues, and I said I would admit to occasionally using the word b**** because women themselves seem to use it proudly. He said he never uses that word. Today in fact I had a rare occasion to use it when I was walking home from the store. I walk slowly nowadays because I an elderly and feel fatigued lately and dizzy at times. Just as I was turning left on the sidewalk to approach my apartment, a small young lady rushed by to my left, slamming up against me much to my surprise.

I exclaimed "Whoa, hold your horses young lady."

She responded with "f*** you old man."

"I was only joking."

"F*** you."

"Hey, don't be such a b****, I said I was only joking, and you surprised me because you didn't say excuse me before you tried to pass."

"Go back to your country."

"Okay, but please do not be such a b****."

"You're just an old man," she shouted as she walked away.

"Hey, don't be such a b****, b****."

To which she yelled back over her shoulder "go back to Cuba."

"Well I'm not Cuban and I have never been to Cuba, but I have lived here probably twice your age, and I am advising you don't be such a b**** b**** because if you do you're not going to like what's going to happen to you."

I wonder if she is a South Beach b**** because I have never encountered anyone like her here over the years. She couldn't be from New York because New Yorkers say "excuse me" before slamming into you. Maybe it has something to do with the Super Bowl this weekend or the way the stars are aligned. I gave her some good advice, and I hope she takes it because if she does her life will go better.

I told my friend what happened.

"More effective response to that girl should have been "you f****** b****" And, when she said go back to your country, your response should have been, "I am in my country you f****** c***."

"No thanks. I am not a p****."

How Many Press Heralds Do Gods Have?

"The details are in my story," said Martin Vassolo, the Miami Herald beat reporter for Miami Beach.

"Thank the Herald, messenger of the Gods, for that!" I exclaimed.

"No, I'm just a guy trying to do his best to inform the public."

A messenger does not write the messages he delivers. A guy doing his best to inform the public must form those stories for his newspaper, even if inspired by the gods above him.

The public is often misinformed by the particular selection of facts and the biases and prejudices of reporters, editors, and publishers. Of course a newspaper cannot be all things to all people, and it would choke to death on muck if it tried to rake it all up. The Miami Herald has many merits, yet I have noticed several faults after my encounter with its executive editor there, the highly esteemed Tom Fiedler, who left the paper in 2007 and became dean of Boston University's College of communication.

He announced his retirement from the University in 2019 and said he intended to go to work for Cory Booker's presidential campaign because, like Teddy Roosevelt, he wanted to be a man with a cause. "I made the decision that I am not going back to journalism. I don't have the discipline," he explained in an interview for the university press. "I'm too caught up right now and my own believe that the current situation in our country has to change to go back and be objective about it."

His worst critics then charged him with the degradation of his profession and the rise of Donald Trump and other political figures despite salacious scandals. He would insist in a November 20, 2018 Boston University Today interview that he was misrepresented in the 'Front Runner,' a movie about Senator Gary Hart's 1998 presidential campaign, for which he broke the story of the candidates infidelity when he was with the Miami Herald.

The event itself allegedly became a turning point for political campaign coverage. He was apparently insulted by the depiction of his handsome self as an unkempt journalist. The movie was inaccurate, he said, smeared him, and might damage the university's reputation, but he declined to sue. He said the most glaring factual error was that he had hung up on a tipster before she provided information, but he said he actually had two long conversations that provided enough information to confront Senator Hart about his relationship with Donna Rice, a Miami woman, on that fateful night in Washington DC. No, he claimed, the reporting was not an epochal change of reporters' behavior. The big story just happened to put a spotlight on it. He said his story just boiled down to the facts, a tip upon which a reporter verifies and writes a story. The political issue was hypocrisy.

All that was of interest to me because Mr. Fiedler had informed me before he left the Miami Herald that, "a complex calculus comes into play in choosing columnists—market need, experience, reputation, credibility in a subject, demographics profile (i.e. race, gender and ethnicity)—that goes beyond the ability to write well. Some excellent writers simply never get a column because they're in the unfortunate position of not being the right something-or-other to suit the papers needs at the time when an opening occurs."

I obviously do not qualify for a column at that paper given its complex requirements and my dissatisfaction with how it addresses market needs.

I recall that Arthur M. Simon, a Florida banking official whom I interviewed at the University of Miami, was wrongly cast by the Miami Herald as a chief villain in its 2009 award-winning series on the Allen Stanford fraud. The editors failed to make retractions after the potentially libelous errors were pointed out.

I also remember that Miami Herald reporter Patricia Mazzei professed ignorance of various corrupt practices that had been referred to Miami Herald reporters including herself. Her "We didn't know about it" was greeted by guffaws at a meeting for "citizen journalists" held by the ethics Commission in 2012. The director at the time, former state corruption prosecutor "Sleeping Joe" Centorino, who maintained a cozy relationship with City of Miami Beach attorneys for many years, was rewarded recently with the post of Miami Beach's first Inspector General.

And there was the Tennis Center Fiasco, during which the Miami Herald beat reporter said he was too bored by the constant allegations of corruption, drug-dealing, and embezzlement in Miami Beach to report the details. Moreover, serious allegations of racketeering involving the building and Fire Departments of Miami Beach were ignored by the Miami Herald until someone was actually arrested. And during the Espanola Way Affair, the Miami

Herald pulled a reporter off of an investigation of Mayor Philip Levine's possible complicity in the persecution of a whistleblowing tenant by the mayor's partner, the owner of the complex.

Moreover, the Miami Herald ignored calls for the full reporting of Miami Beach crime statistics and continued its practice of publishing the city's reports on constantly diminishing major crime numbers that would eventually have given the number of crimes as less than zero.

More recently, in the Sadigo Affair, the city manager, city attorneys, the mayor and commissioners, many of them lawyers, turned a blind eye to an allegation by Miami Beach hotelier Rod Eisenberg at an open commission meeting that a city attorney had suborned the perjury of a key witness in a short-term rental prosecution. To the best of my knowledge, Mayor Dan Gelber and several commissioners refused to see Mr. Eisenberg prior to that testimony, and the allegations and evidence were not subsequently referred to the US Attorney and the Florida Bar; that raises questions of possible misprision of felony and attorney misconduct. The Miami Herald was notified in advance of the meeting and the details but did not report on it.

Yet everywhere was "The Herald" considered as the one and only authoritative news source. So I created an internet journal called the South Beach Herald to play a little joke on the Miami Herald. I contacted possible news sources when I wanted to know something, and I said I was "Walters with the herald." There was, incidentally, a guy named Walters at the Miami Herald. My sources, thinking there was only one Herald in the world, not to mention the Boston Herald, the Chicago Herald, the Albany Herald, and so on, often got right back to me and spilled the beans. That was usually the last time they did so if they discovered who I was, a wild-card who could not be controlled rather than a cooperative member of the so-called legitimate press, that is, the fourth branch of government, or rather part of its bureaucracy, for the good reason that it is indeed part of and dependent on the government for news and is not the beholden to the public except to its advertisers.

A Greek Herald was not only "some guy trying to do his best to inform the public" of what had happened; he was also a harbinger who told people of what was to come, marshalled militant forces to protect it from enemies, and praised heroes who excelled in that task. A herald, then, would protect the public from inimical government rather than being a branch of it.

Mention is made of heralds in ancient literature. We learn from the 'Judgment of Paris,' the tale of a classic beauty contest, that Hera ("protectress"), the heroic goddess of women, marriage and childbirth, hated the Trojans because Paris, a Trojan mortal, had decided that Aphrodite, who offered him the most beautiful woman in the world as a bribe, was more beautiful than her and Athena, whose bribe was skill in war. Therefore Hera, who had offered Paris the kingdom of Asia as her bribe, indignantly supported the Greeks in their battles with the Trojan Army. She call upon Stentor, a general with stentorian voice, to inspire the Greeks.

"For who can be the general of such a vast multitude," asked Aristotle in Politics, "or who the herald, unless he have the voice of Stentor?" Homer's Iliad recounted the event: "When they came to the place where the bravest and most in number were gathered about mighty Diomedes, fighting like lions or wild boars of great strength and endurance, there Hera stood still and raised a shout like that of brazen-voiced Stentor, whose cry was as loud as that of 50 men together. "Argives," she cried, "shame on cowardly creatures, brave in semblance only as long as Achilles was fighting, his spirit so deadly that the Trojans dared not show themselves outside the Dardanian gates, but now they sally far from the city and fight even at your ships.' With these words she put heart and soul into them all." (Homer: Iliad 5.785)

Hermes, messenger of the gods, protector of heralds, travelers, merchants, thieves and orators became the Herald of heralds after he won a shouting contest with Stentor, who then died. Hermes confess to the theft of some oxen, and was duly awarded winged sandals to facilitate travel between divine and mortal spheres. His Roman likeness is Mercury (merx, merchandise) God of eloquence, messages, and trade. Mind you that the gods have all the faults of mortals but mortality, if that be a fault instead of a blessing.

So, in commemoration of ancient mythology, a newspaper might be called the Crier, the Bawler, the Messenger, the Shouter, The Courier and so on. And, in a herald's capacity as an indicator of things to come, it might be named the Harbinger, the Forecaster, the Prognosticator, and the like. Since newspaper owners and editors often think of their publications as public-spirited instruments dedicated to the progress of their communities, and therefore support persons they believe are praiseworthy, the Booster, the Apologist, the Extoller, The Advocate, and so on might come to mind, and then we have the

Advertiser that sings praises of goods for a fee.

So-called legitimate journalists are nowadays expected to be carefully conditioned in college and to hold relatively low-paid jobs for some time before they can be trusted to express opinions and columns and perhaps go on to become executive editors and university professors like Mr. Fiedler. Therefore my opinion as an autodidact is worthless to Publishers. Nevertheless, I am moved to express it from time to time as if I were a columnist with a message from the gods.

If It's Brown Put It Down

I was astonished when a friend told me it was a damn shame that an elderly man such as me had been attacked on the street in front of Crunch Fitness South Beach. I have never considered myself as elderly although as a child I thought I might be thousands of years old, so I resented people when they called me a little boy at my foster home in Muskogee. I was also astonished when Tanya Savage at Crunch presented me with a certificate for physical therapy to help with my back, which I wrenched when I threw the heavy man who jumped on me onto the sidewalk.

I was inclined to decline the gift because being independent is my forte: I am more afraid of being dependent than of death itself. But I accepted it because Tanya is beautiful and sincere, and I remembered the Polynesian custom of accepting a gift: failing to do so would insult the giver. One chief had actually spat upon the pots, pans and mirrors the white man had brought to the island and laid out on a blanket. "We have our own things," said the chief, which was to say, "F*** you haole."

I was unable to stand and walk for two days after the incident, but I am mobile once again. The training sessions with Phillip Carrington at the fitness club, albeit painful, have been helpful. I am worried that I may wind up in a wheelchair or a walker, which for me would be worse than death. My father hobbled along without a walker until his death at ninety because, he said, "After they give you a walker they want to warehouse you and take away your social security."

Yesterday I heard a woman screaming "Ayudame, ayudame!" I went outside and looked in between the buildings. There she lay on the sidewalk beside her walker. That reminded me of the advertisement for the notification device in the ad that warns people it is disturbing because an elderly woman was at the bottom of the stairs with her laundry crying, "Please help me, I've fallen."

My elderly neighbor was not hurt badly, just a scraped knee. She refused my offer to call 911.She said she had Medicare, but had a terrible experience when an ambulance came on a previous occasion.

My back still hurt, she was heavy, and lifting her back onto her walker was difficult. I got her into the elevator and into her apartment after considerable fiddling with her big ring of keys because she had trouble remembering which was which so I had to try them all. I noticed the elevator did not have a safety mechanism to keep the door open in case someone tried to stop it from closing by thrusting their arm into while it was closing.

Her English was minimal, and my Spanish is pathetic. I guessed correctly that her first name is Maria. She laughed when I said all Hispanic women are called Maria. She called her daughter from her phone inside the apartment, and then told me her daughter was drunk at her birthday party and would not come to help. I cleaned and bandaged her scraped knee, then left her because she could move around, and she said she had a helper coming in the morning, but would call me if she was in trouble.

I emailed Captain de Espriella for advice. He takes good care of our neighborhood. If only his chief were not so liberal it would be even better. He promised to have someone look in upon her the next day and to get her social services if she needed it, as she is hardly able to walk.

A neighbor of mine said that Maria does have a maid coming in every day except on Sunday, and on Sundays she tends to go outside for a walk and often falls down and it's very difficult to get her home. The whole thing seems to be a ritual. Then her building manager said the poor lady gets tipsy, and I recalled the first thing the woman had done when I got her home was to offer me a drink. I may be thousands of years old myself, and I think I can remember the dinosaur days, yet my spirit always seems relatively young compared to eternity. My body is obviously coming undone, and rather suddenly at that. I do not want to look into mirrors anymore. No one is going to call me little boy again, that much is for sure, though now that I think of it again, I am still that little boy. I'm sure everyone knows what I mean though they might not admit it.

Oh how my back ached this morning! Maybe my mattress, which I retrieved from the alley ten years ago, is making matters worse. The quality of discards in the alleys is going down in South Beach so I may write an essay on whether that is a sign of advance or decline of the quality of life. Beds cost a fortune; if I spend my life savings on one, my fortune would be wasted because rich people are buying up properties, rents are going through the roof, and we expect to be evicted soon. I would try to sleep on the hard floor if it were not for the huge palmetto bugs that pass through from time to time no matter what kind of cockroach spray one uses.

The game is obviously almost over, I realized once again as I looked at the wall, the wall I call death. Hopefully I will hit it in my sleep during a sweet dream, and my body will be taken away and cremated after they find the notification card in my wallet advising to cremate right away. I apologize in advance for the odor causing my body to be found, because nobody will miss me enough to inquire in the first place, which is my own fault, of course, for in America everyone but God is to blame for their fate. I chose to be an independent, honest author instead of money-grubbing writer. Honesty does not pay in this country; when I do tell the truth, which can be rather complicated, I am called a liar.

Oh how I regret nobody will bother forgiving me for my sins, and that I am not the gentleman I should be. I have managed to disgust myself after listening to people demean me. Maybe I could figure out how to commit suicide on the Internet, I thought, put down a plastic sheet under the chair, or why not a plastic bag over my head? Well, I am not suicidal, my back hurts, but things are not really as bad as they seem....

I finally got up from my mattress sideways so as not to aggravate my back. At least that is a positive step, I thought, and I admitted to myself I am not a good philosopher because according to Socrates wise men gladly consider death as a matter of habit. The purpose of life, after all, is death. I resolved to try to think of something else in the interim since my procreative days have passed along with a great deal of foolishness.

I affirmed that it was going to be a very nice day. I resolved to stop feeling old, to go to the homeless folk library and use the fancy new computers to avoid my own truth by researching other people's problems. I stopped by the Burger King for their excellent Arabic coffee along the way, and as I was sitting there, a Hispanic woman wearing jewelry approached me and offered me her hash browns. She evidently thought that I am a poor old perhaps homeless man reading my book, which happened to be Karl Marx's account of the Paris Commune because I love French history and dream of visiting France because prophets are not recognized at home and French people are revolutionary.

It occurred to me that I may have looked destitute because I was wearing brown. My friend Elizabeth warned me, that when looking in the closet for clothes to wear, if they are brown, put them down. If she had known about this lady wearing jewelry, she probably would have advised me to go home with her.

No, I am not thousands of years old, after all. I am going to take all my brown clothes, given to me by bereaved or divorced women, and put them in the alley for the homeless people living there.

South Beach Psychophant

I did not approve of the rehabilitation of South Pointe Park at first. I made an exception for the Lifeguard Lighthouse on the beach, but I did not care for the staggered column of the lighthouse sculpture now surrounded by dog waste in the park. Ironically, my father's ashes were scattered in the water nearby before it became a protested dog park. He did not care much for dogs himself; he said they should be canned and shipped to the Philippines to feed the poor.

As for the faux iceberg sculptures capping off the restrooms in the park, I thought they represented the frozen hearts of phony politicians who forced the renovation down the throats of frustrated conservatives.

However, I have had a change of heart. I even recommended to Mayor Philip 'King' Levine that the park be renamed after Jorge Gonzalez, the ousted city manager who oversaw the project. Sadly, that cannot be done until he is dead and permanent gone; his return is feared by the current regime, faux reformists who advocated welcome changes, some of whom may have secretly wished him dead. I have often enjoyed South Pointe Park since his departure even though the walkway has become too crowded during my Sunday morning walks. But its popularity among the gentility, who are better off than the *gentuza* who fished there before, has provided me with the opportunity to cover two robberies around the icebergs in the last three Sundays. Of course there is always a story to be told about something wherever I go.

I espied two women photographing a model in his blue underpants on the iceberg deck last Sunday. It was suitably icy on the deck so all but he were warmly clad. He lacked the prerequisite of barbarian comeliness: a hirsute physique notwithstanding a bald pate evidencing abundant testosterone.

Barbarians, as we know, hail from the north, where they were created by the iceberg gods. Most men, since they left jungle and forest, prefer their females rather hairless, and small for the sake of portability, hence evolution has rendered them relatively small and hairless in comparison to males, whose brute power gave them no cause to shed their own hair but to flaunt it and grow in stature. Conservative men certainly do not remove from their bodies what little hair they may have been blessed with, a fact that is greatly appreciated by a tactile Cherokee woman I met on a train from Chicago to New York City back in the good old days when I let my undergrowth run wild.

"Do you ladies need a model with a hairy chest, hairy legs, and hairy belly?" I asked the photographers, but they demurred, and their model giggled. What is this world coming to?

Maybe I complain too much. I admit that I have complained a lot about the present state of many things, therefore my objections to change unless they are my changes are hypocritical. I have learned from the admission of my own hypocrisy in comparison to others that hypocrisy is the underlying crisis of human nature. We are not all that we would be, and we are moved to lie about who we are and to complain about what other people do or do not do.

In fact, complaining is the lever of human progress, so people are welcome to blame me for complaining, especially about government, and to send me one dollar each. My dad said, understandingly, that I had a "conflict with authority." We all have a bit of that, without which we would not be a people destined for freedom in order.

Now in the old days, those of the Athenian democracy, there were no regular public prosecutors. Citizens called *indices*, *denuntiatores*, and *delators* could volunteer to file informations or complaints on behalf of the public. It was said private wrongs resulted in public goods. We democrats have not changed much since Athens. Now that an official sniveler has threatened to slap me with a defamation suit for doing what he has done to me, I sympathize with the predicament Aeschines spoke of in his speech against Timarchus, and am fain to defend myself:

"I have never, fellow citizens, brought indictment against any Athenian, nor vexed any man when he was rendering account of his office; but in all such matters I have, as I believe, shown myself a quiet and modest man. But when I saw that the city was being seriously injured by the defendant, Timarchus, who, though disqualified by law, was speaking in your assemblies [he later argues that Timarchus should have been disqualified by unethical behavior from practicing law], and when I myself was made a victim of his blackmailing attack the nature of the attack I will show in the course of my speech, I decided that it would be a most shameful thing if 1 failed to come to the defense of the whole city and its laws, and to your defense and my own; and knowing that he was liable to the accusations that you heard read a moment ago by the clerk of the court, I instituted this suit, challenging him to official scrutiny. Thus it appears, fellow citizens, that what is so frequently said of public suits is no mistake, namely, that very often *private enmities correct public abuses*."

In any case, if someone simply had a grudge against someone back then for which there was no civil remedy, he could sue him for some crime or the other. Of course that process was abused by informers called "sycophants" for giving the finger or "showing the fig" to someone while flattering the public that they were taking action for its good.

Now I admit that I have shown the fig to various authorities including local officials of the City of Miami Beach, lately in the form of sign code violations on every block, but not because I consider any official in particular as an enemy with whom I must get even. Mind you that it is they who have threatened to bring frivolous and malicious suits against me to shut me up.

The public naturally suspected that sycophants had ulterior motives, that they were wont to bring frivolous and malicious suits against their personal enemies. Aristophanes took them to task in his comedy named after the god of wealth, *Plutus*, in dialogue between Good Man and Informer.

Informer admitted to Good Man that he had no occupation other than being the caretaker of public and private affairs by informing the public of wrongdoing. My own version of Good Man, the city attorney or city sphinx who guards the city walls with sophisms, publicly compared me to an unemployed, unlicensed watchdog that stalks public officials and urinates in city-hall's hallways.

Yet I, like the ancient comic poet's Informer, naturally perceive myself to be one of the more honest and patriotic citizens of *my* cosmos. Just Man asks how Informer can be of any benefit by meddling in other people's business, and Informer replies that he does not meddle but rather benefits the public by supporting enacted laws by not permitting them to be broken. Well, are not judges appointed to handle litigation? Yes, but anyone who wishes can prosecute, answers our sycophant, and that person is me because I am concerned with affairs of state. Good Man then concludes that the state has a bad patron.

The modern state saved itself from such bad patrons by providing cooperative sycophants with a monopoly on the practice of law. Lawyers, sycophants for the power elite, are licensed to extort and blackmail and defame people at will, and it is nearly impossible to hold them liable for abuse of process and malicious prosecution provided that they flatter the public with their noble pretensions to save it from perdition with their sophistry.

South Beach Journalist Cleared of Goofballing

Florida Attorney General Pam Bondi was presented this month with a copy of a letter addressed to Miami-Dade County Inspector General Patra P.Y. Liu on the subject of permissive permitting practices in the county as well as the ignored or forgiven failure of some owners, developers and contractors to obtain permits at all.

The gist of the letter, authored by David Arthur Walters, was that officials are negligent and perhaps corrupt when it comes to enforcing building permit laws, virtually ignoring information about violations or doing nothing about them in some circumstances.

"As for inspector general reports," Walters told the inspector general, "the public rarely reads them; the few that do say, 'So what?' And law enforcement apparently has bigger fish to fry unless the press fans the flames to scandalous proportions. And it appears that there will be no careful investigation by any of the local, state and federal police powers given their limitations and their emphasis on compliance over punishment, which is one reason that compliance lags.'

Walters said that the local inspector general has declined to investigate allegations of official misconduct and gross negligence in Miami Beach for want of resources. The City of Miami Beach is plagued by corruption and arrests. Several of its departments have been publicly maligned as "RICO operations" by a fire inspector named David Weston, who believes he was fired for insisting that millions of dollars in permit fees had gone missing. Newly hired City Manager Jimmy Morales has promised to address the City Commission on that subject.

Walters opined, based on his investigation of an errant general contractor's projects, that the City of Miami Beach is far better than the City of Miami when it comes to enforcement of building and licensing regulations. Miami Beach recently hired Mariano Fernandez, Miami's former building director, to cure its problems. Walters said he had been naïve at the outset of his investigations, but was soon informed that "Everybody Does It, Everybody Knows It, and Nobody Cares." Samantha Santana, responding for the Attorney

General, said Ms. Bondi had received a copy of Walters' letter to the local inspector general, and asked her to respond to it.

"Section 16.01(3), Florida Statutes, which sets forth the powers and duties of the Attorney General's Office, authorizes our office to provide legal opinions and statutory interpretations to public officials on questions of law pertaining to their own official duties. This precludes us from giving legal opinions or advice to private individuals. However, I hope the following information proves helpful. You should continue to work with your local city officials and county inspector general's office to address any information or evidence you have regarding your concerns. If you are concerned about conflicts of interest or ethics involving public officials, you may contact the Governor's Office and the Commission on Ethics."

Walters replied that he was not expecting legal advice from Ms. Bondi on what he called "the swamp of iniquity confronting honest citizens in South Florida. I hoped that she would be willing to examine, in her capacity as the chief legal officer and the chief law enforcement officer of the State of Florida under the Florida Constitution, and as an attorney bound by professional ethics standards that promote integrity beyond the interests of her client, a great deal of information from various sources that would cause a reasonable lay person to believe that something is systemically wrong with the exercise of the police power in South Florida at least, and then provide her honest opinion to the governor and others, without being asked for her advice, as to what action should be taken if any. In the event she decided to take a look at such information.

"I am not the only one who would furnish reports that demonstrate that all local avenues for redress of grievances have been exhausted by official neglect if not moral and criminal corruption, and how that promotes contempt for government. Relief is intermittently provided by the federal government including the F.B.I., but it is my opinion that such interventions would be unnecessary if preventive measures would be taken to reform what some professional investigators say is the corruption of capital of the nation."

He complained that so many opinions are issued by the Attorney General, to the effect that no advice can be given except the advice to contact the very officials whose neglect was complained about, that "anyone seeking a remedy feels like a ping-pong ball bouncing between the levels and departments of government, and in doing so appear to the officials to be goofballs for persevering in their quest."

Of course if mainstream media decides that the issue into a matter of great public importance, for example the deceptive manner in which respectable attorneys were handling foreclosures, the Attorney General will be able to tell you exactly how many complaints were filed with her office and what she tried to do about it before banging her head on bench and bar.

"I recall a woman suffering from Legal Abuse Syndrome—she was abused by Brevard County lawyers and judges: She thought the Governor was responsible for upholding the laws of the state. However, when she appeared at his office she was ushered out, and had the presence of mind to go home lest she be committed to a mental hospital, as was done in the USSR upon determination of Sluggish Schizophrenia, or failure to realize that the Soviet government was the best possible government. Ms. Bondi, who recommends people back to the very local authorities complained of might appreciate the remark made by a woman regarding advice to complain to the local chains-of-command when raped in the military: Complaining to the chain-of-command, she said, is like telling your father that your brother raped you."

When contacted and asked if he was a goofball, Walters said, in a 5,700-word written response, that the term was suggested to him by David Weston, who had also blessed him with the observation that City Attorney Jose Smith is a Magic Eight Ball. Weston, he said, had contacted him with his tale, which he said he found entirely credible based on the supporting documentation, but he said Weston then tried to manipulate the investigative process and the drafting of his reports in every way.

"He sent our email along with lengthy commentary and explanations to the editor of the SunPost, to whom I did not intend to submit anything, and he interceded in communications with officials to either 'apologize' for me or disagree with my opinions, and he finally implied that I was a 'goofball' in reference to my letter to the Attorney General."

Walters said that he and Weston had had a philosophical difference from the beginning: He felt that the problem with the city government was the managers themselves, who should be removed and replaced with outsiders, while Weston believed the issue was their management style, which he wanted to help change and thus become part of the solution, saying that if only management had listened to him previously, there would have been no F.B.I. arrests and families suffering as a consequence.

"Weston is right about the city's mismanagement of his own case," Walters declared, "but I must say that I felt like firing him. He writes well himself, so why did enlist me? Because he thought I would get his story into the SunPost. Anyway, people can call me whatever they want. Maybe I am a goofball. A famous blogger called me a gadfly recently. I was flattered although I don't hold a candle to Socrates. A ping pong ball may turn into a goofball or screwball after being batted brainless ad infinitum. Wrong seems right to some people when done long enough, and anyone who believes it is wrong is called 'delusional.' Anyone who insists that all the codes be regularly and evenly enforced must seem to be a goofball to building officials. They like to be liked, and to think of themselves as nice, liberal officials, though in the end they are despised for that. Why, one of them asked me how I expected anything to get done if all the laws were diligently enforced! He asked me where in the world a budget could be found to do that. Especially with new laws are being created every day legislatures do business. Anyway, goofball or not, I sent the stuff along to the governor to see what he calls me."

We contacted Dr. Benjamin Plotkin, a noteworthy expert on political psychology, for his opinion on Walters' transactions with Florida public officials, and whether or not he is a political goofball.

"Ours is not a perfect world," Plotkin said in a written statement. "Voltaire was wrong to satirize Leibniz' perspective. The absolutely perfect world Leibniz had in mind was the substantial world, the City of God, not this material world.

"That being said, I have been following Walters since he arrived in Florida. I find his writings rather typical of intellectuals before they become intelligentsia for the Establishment. I would not call him a goofball but he does goof around from time to time, and that might cause bureaucrats to climb out of the muck for a breath of fresh air and expose faults in the Establishment anonymously.

"He like other frustrated reformers, no matter how cynical, beg askance of the Establishment because they believe people are inherently good hence genuine reform is possible. Pragmatic politicians during the Gilded Age believed men and women of the doubly reformed faith were impractical freaks, sterile dreamers doomed to isolation and extinction if not eternal hellfire. Spiro Agnew thought they were sterile too, that they were impotent, effete snobs.

"Walters might be an excellent muckraking journalist. Hitler was wont to denounce critical journalists on the whole as 'scoundrels.' Disgruntled scribblers can bring down regimes if they chip away long enough. No less than Max Weber pointed out the importance of independent journalists as politicians themselves. But as Eric Hoffer pointed out, dissident writers both love and hate authority. If brought into the fold, they may serve as great apologists for the Establishment. That is what happened to the late A.C. Weinstein in Miami Beach, when he went from the SunPost to work for Mayor Dermer."

The Virtues of Sycophancy

My Dearest Commissioner Kristen Rosen Gonzalez: The gist of the academic essay 'An Adultery' I sent to you, after hearing that you had advocated constructive criticism on the commission instead of inimical personal attacks, was that it is best for critics to paint a better picture than to castigate the one in front of them. I hope you interpreted my offering for its literary sensibility, and not as sexual harassment.

I have today posted in that context an excerpt from my work in progress, *Signs of Madness*, entitled 'My Southe Pointe Parke Psycophancy', the gist of which is that the motive for complaints upon which the progress of our civilization is based are ideals to which reality falls short. I believe one of your colleagues who is a professional sycophant will appreciate that fact as it has been a good source of income to him.

Our commission has suffered recently from an unwitting bout of malignant narcissism in the person of Mayor Philip Levine. Even when constructive suggestions are made by persons not subject to that malady, the suggestion is ignored and the person is impugned, called a "yeller and a screamer."

It is with that in mind that I thank you for your resistance to his antisocial egotism,

David Arthur Walters

Don't miss out!

Visit the website below and you can sign up to receive emails whenever David Arthur Walters publishes a new book. There's no charge and no obligation.

https://books2read.com/r/B-A-VVMQ-JSBTB

BOOKS 2 READ

Connecting independent readers to independent writers.

Also by David Arthur Walters

The Seed That Fell On Rocky Ground
South Beach Florida Coronavirus Panic 2020
The Yellow Vest Movement
Signs of Madness
The Compassionate Heart of America
My Hawaii Nei
The Amazing South Beach HDD Sewer Project
Tracey's Secret
The Amazing Kansas City Library
The Helgalian Chronicles
The Espanola Way of Doing Business
Katherine Sergava
No Hard Feelings - A Dancer's Reflections
Sovereign Immunity - The Debasement of the United States
Helene and Paul - A Characterological Romance
Anarkhia
Random Ramblings
Melange
Ideology aka Idiotology
Accounts Payable - My Life Past Due
The Sly Way Gurdjieff & Ouspensky
Groundhog Days - Timely Intercourse
The Black VIrgin
APXH - Wicked Political Musings
Open Publishing
My Hand

www.ingramcontent.com/pod-product-compliance
Lightning Source LLC
LaVergne TN
LVHW041032150826
845672LV00001B/289
* 9 7 9 8 2 2 7 6 5 3 7 4 1 *